A
KARMIC
ATTRACTION

Liz Hayes and Rhea Gargour

A KARMIC ATTRACTION

WE ARE KMB LTD
63-66 Hatton Garden
London, EC1N 8LE

ISBN number paperback: 978-1-7393783-3-2
ISBN number ebook: 978-1-7393783-4-9

КMB

.

Table of Contents

"There are two ways of spreading light: to be the candle or the mirror that reflects it."

—Edith Wharton

Shit Happens
Rhea

"Fuck This."

Those two words were my salvation. It may sound strange, especially for the start of a book that appears to be about spirituality, but that phrase was one of the most divine things I had ever uttered.

My life was fine. I had a roof over my head, people who loved me, and pockets of laughter tinged with (a sort of) happiness. Thing is, I also had moments of desperation, shame, heartbreak, and emptiness that no amount of someone else's energy could fill. But I was coping. I bargained with my hopelessness, desperately looking for a better tomorrow whilst also running away from the past. I told myself to grin and bear it, and I convinced myself that it was okay that things in my life weren't quite working out because they weren't totally falling apart. Life was hard for everyone, and I was lucky that it wasn't harder for me. I may have had my desires and dreams, but I also had the reality check that I was unlikely to realize them in my lifetime.

"Fuck This."

I was done pretending I was okay whilst secretly waiting for the next disappointment, the next hurdle, or the next punishment that would remind me that survival was the best I could hope for. I was done existing in the never-ending loop of my mind, trying to figure out what I'd done wrong, what I was doing wrong, and what I could do to prevent being wrong again. I was done neglecting my needs and desires in order to cope. And I was definitely done dismantling the connection between who I was and who I was pretending to be.

"Fuck This."

In lieu of knowing what else to do (for the first time in many, many years), I went to the gym. That was the first miracle. The second miracle was making a friend who could chat with the universe over a coffee (yep, she hears MANY voices and apparently they're pretty knowledgeable). When I found out what Liz could do (she practices a craft called Soul Memory Discovery—more on that later), I had a session as quickly as I could, not knowing what would come next.

What came next was the opportunity to ask the questions that I'd been too scared to ask for so long; not only in that session but through our friendship and ultimately through the podcast we recorded together in her utility closet, *Karma's My Bitch*. As a result, we got the answers to my questions, as well as many others—all the while allowing it all to unfold in this magical way that we couldn't have predicted.

Thing is, to change my life, I had to understand that the responsibility was mine alone. Some exhilarating breakthroughs were preceded by difficult breakdowns.

Some amazing payoffs were preceded by terrifying risks. But every moment was priceless because of where I ended up.

Not only do I experience life differently, but I also see myself differently, and so do the others who interact with me. I have had more fun and joy than I ever thought possible, I have done things that I never thought I could, and I have experienced so much more beauty than I thought I deserved.

As you may have guessed by now, I'm not here to talk about spirituality in the way it's usually taught. I'm also not here to preach about science or faith. When I needed to understand why things weren't working out, science was too general, faith was too personal, and spirituality was a minefield.

To me, karma is just a fancy word for something far simpler: the Shit that happens that hurts, the Shit that forces us to grow up in some way, or the Shit that forces us to make a choice that either brings us back to ourselves or pushes us further away from who we are. Whoever we are, whoever we pretend to be, from whatever walk of life we've taken and whatever experiences we've had, there is one undeniable truth: Shit happens to everyone. Our time in that utility closet (and beyond) taught us why Shit happens and what to do about it.

In this book, you will hear from both Liz and me (Rhea). Some of the pages tell our story and show the moments, experiences, and realizations that transformed everything. The others are the concepts and teachings that serve as the larger spiritual theory to which they correspond. The chapters within this book follow the episodes of our podcast. Even though the lessons came through the podcast first (keen eyes will notice that we reference the names of the episodes throughout), we explain them here in more detail.

Together, we hope to give you the full picture of why this work is so important and how it helps us transcend the Shit that happens. It's why we wrote this book; the wisdom and work are too precious for us to keep to ourselves.

We all have the power to change our world. It's just that sometimes our Shit gets in the way.

Life's a Bitch
Liz

Beneath all the superficial differences among us, there lies one thing that we all have in common. This common thread is *why* we're all so fucking lost, unhappy, isolated, and running in circles while trying to escape. We may not recognize what we're running from, but we can't seem to help it. We jump from job to job, relationship to relationship, place to place, drama to drama, lamenting, complaining, and wondering why the Shit in our lives doesn't get better or only improves incrementally despite all our efforts.

We can't stop running away from this thing, this nagging feeling, thought, or issue that's always been there. We feel compelled to stay one step ahead of it, even though we can't quite identify it. We would all like to stop running, to be able to catch our breath and end our suffering. Yet, the rub is that it doesn't end.

No matter what we do, those feelings, thoughts, and issues remain. Same problem, different day. We become the victims in our own stories. The woe-is-me, nothing-good-ever-happens-to-me, life-sucks-and-then-you-die, and why-me sentiments fill us with a torrent of emotions, often leading to further regret and sorrow.

This is why we often "shoulda, coulda, woulda" every life event as we lie awake at night wishing things would've gone another way. It's also why we try to micromanage, control, and anticipate all the possible outcomes to ensure a different one happens next time. We tell ourselves to let go, be grateful, and be mindful. We bookmark deep quotes, post inspiring passages, and recite pithy self-help mantras like "live your best life," "you are worth it," "you deserve the best," "never settle," and "find someone who values you."

We look to influencers and self-proclaimed experts to remind us what we want to so desperately believe about ourselves but deep down can't. This leaves us with FOMO (the fear of missing out) and a feeling that everyone else is doing way better than we are—all the while, self-doubt, deep-seated fears, and imposter syndrome plague us.

This self-help coping mechanism is just one of many we turn to. Drugs (illegal or prescription), alcohol, gambling, exercise, religion, sex, and codependent relationships are among the many things we engage in to assuage our nagging fears that we can barely outpace. But the greatest coping mechanism of all is blame.

If we're a victim in our story, we need a perpetrator or an antagonist. The childhood trauma; our mother; our father; our siblings; our third-grade teacher; the bully in school; being dumped by our first, second, or third love; not getting cast as a lead in a play; not getting into our first-choice university; not getting the job we wanted; the break-up we didn't see coming; not getting the cutout life we thought we should have… The list goes on and on and on. Like a movie reel that plays in our minds, we go through each and every life event, leading to ever-growing resentment and a sense of powerlessness in this perpetrator–victim cycle.

But our feelings, those nagging ones that are informed by our fears that shit will go south and that our issues can be fixed by someone else's profound thoughts, tell us to play it safe by making calculated, predictable choices. As a result, we lead lives out of harmony with who we really are.

We may toy with self-destructive behaviors yet run home to the safety of our beds, soul-sucking jobs with mediocre paychecks, partners we don't love, or lovers who aren't capable of loving us when it becomes too much. And we have no idea who the fuck we actually are because we have become so far removed from that person by building walls to keep our original self safe, a person who seemed weak and unable to cope with life.

It's this powerlessness that we have been forced to confront throughout our lives, erasing our feelings of safety and security. But life on Earth was never meant to be safe and secure. That doesn't mean that life sucks until we die. Rather, it's that life *might* suck until we figure out *why*. That's been the point all along.

Bad Bitch

We cannot make our Shit better until we understand *why* it's happening, which is the catch-22 of our lives. When we're trying to grasp the *why*, it often requires a spiritual lens to get the most expanded perspective. This is because it offers the largest view that we, as humans, are capable of having.

The *why* is quite simply karma, although not as it's been commonly understood—you know, the old adage: "What goes around comes around." Karma isn't just a bitch, it is *the* bitch; the inescapable bitch that has us spinning around, chasing our tails through every life event, and wondering why we can't make our Shit better.

Sure, maybe we developed enough backbone or self-esteem to dump the cheater, only then to wind up with another cheater, and we can't fathom why. Maybe we changed jobs, assuming it was our manager, the hours, the mundane work, or coworkers that made it difficult, only to realize the next place we landed was the same story. Whatever it is, whatever is happening, it's always karma because karma is underpinned by the fear that we are not *good enough*.

Karma is not just a belief that can be disbelieved through mental training, mindfulness, or positive mantras. If that were the case, many more people would have burned out their karma by now and imposter syndrome wouldn't really be a thing. Instead, it is a deeply wound fear that has permeated our entire beings down to the cellular and spiritual level, which is the reason it has been so inescapable. We are wired to believe, think, feel, know, and fear that we are not *good enough*.

That is a lot for one person to bear. To wake up to it at once would be the death of us. So karma keeps at us relentlessly, giving us opportunity after opportunity to see our fear reflected back to us—not in order to reinforce that fear and make us feel like crap all the time but to get us to burn out that fear and become aware of who we really are. Even if we trained ourselves to act differently and secured a different outcome, that wouldn't burn out the fear; rather, it would keep the fear alive, driving us to outpace that fear by controlling and modifying our behavior.

Dealing with our karma demands, however, as much objectivity and as little judgment as possible. Because while something may not make sense to our seeing-is-believing rational minds, it doesn't mean it isn't valid. It merely requires our willingness to hold a variety of truths simultaneously, accepting that there are myriad possibilities and explanations for what we are seeing, experiencing, feeling, and accepting.

It is not about trading a certain set of beliefs for another, nor is it about adopting a different worldview. Rather, it's about holding a view that is so broad and all-encompassing that we can see everything and everyone with the greatest clarity. This is how consciousness works; and the more conscious we become—that is, the less fear informs how we live and the choices we make—the easier it becomes to live free of fear. (That's really how letting go works too.)

That's why karma is a simple concept. It's the process by which our single fear, *I Am not Good Enough*, plays out. And while it's a bitch, we make it *our* bitch when we confront it and burn out that fear.

What is a little less simple is the *what* because this fear resides at the spiritual and cellular level, and understanding its source may be a stretch for our minds that operate in survival mode. As a result, our response is to either shut it out (coping mechanisms, here we come!) or prove it wrong.

Karma isn't about our survival because it is not a human concept, it's a spiritual one, which means it doesn't threaten or hold judgment. It just *is*. Ultimately, karma is a choice. We either accept and work with it or we don't. That's why many don't come to it until, like Rhea, they are so fed up and frustrated and have literally tried everything under the sun first. Yet, our lives don't necessarily depend on whether or not we take on our karma, but our happiness does. Life sucks and then you die—or life *might* suck until we figure out *why*.

With that level of clarity comes an objectivity we haven't been able to hold before because our thoughts and belief systems have been governed by a polarity which teaches us that there is good and bad, right and wrong, and virtue and vice. As a result, everything and everyone in our world exists within this narrow, bifurcated spectrum (which Rhea and I call Separation).

Working through our karma is a multi-layered process precisely because of this world of Separation. It would be much easier to release ourselves from our karma and burn out our fear if we lived in a vacuum and didn't have to contend with it. It isn't just the internal battle being waged within, it's the external one, too, since our external world of Separation is the mirror of our internal one. And holy hell, what a fight it is. So while we have been so inclined to fight the external forces of Separation for eons (battling evil, standing up to the Goliath of our age), this is the age in which we have grown conscious enough to see that unless we transform and heal our internal world of Separation and end karma once and for all, our outside one will continue to, well, just suck.

And it does suck. Because life sucks and then you die—or life *might* suck until we figure out *why*. Karma is the tough-love teacher that doesn't let us out of the classroom until we've learned all the lessons and completed all of our homework. It's the one thing that wants us to succeed, to ensure that we are truly liberated from our baggage and prepared to live the lives of our choosing the moment we step off campus.

The work required to live that life is like moving through primary and high school in a matter of weeks. It pushes us to grow up. It pushes us to face ourselves and our mistakes. It pushes us to the brink of our sorrow until we think we can't take it anymore. It pushes and pushes us because it is why we are here in body and why it exists. Because if we cannot grow the fuck up and become *adults* in the true meaning of the word—and take complete responsibility for our lives—then the game of consciousness, the very reason we are here, cannot be realized. And then we are left holding the bag for this Shit life for the rest of our lives.

While this might sound dramatic, we only need to look at our world since 2012 to see what this means. We are shocked and dismayed by our world steeped in Separation, but these are merely all the unpleasant parts that we've chosen to ignore (pick any story at any time of day featured on any media outlet). They are the vestiges of our karmic realities that have played out over lifetimes, showing us what a life of polarity and judgment does when left in the hands of naive children. So, to make our world different, we must make ourselves different. We have to cast off our ignorance and confront all the ways in which we've remained willfully blind to our own reality and conformed to others' standards and demands.

Of course, it's understandable that we'd bury our heads in the sand. If we believe that we are not *good enough* to change our circumstances, we can't possibly feel empowered to change our lives, let alone our own world. Instead, it's easier to hand what little power we have over to someone else or some other entity who promises to take care of us, one who has our best interests at heart and vows to put us first. But this is why we not only remain trapped in our karma but why it's such a bitch slap. Because if it's one thing that karma doesn't allow, it's for us to live in our victimhood.

To be able to work with karma and make it *our* bitch, we have to take responsibility for all the choices we made that have landed us where we are, most often on our ass or our face. Moreover, karma pushes us to be accountable to ourselves for all the ways in which we have contributed to our own misery. And this is what hurts the most—to realize that we haven't acted in our best interest and that we have been complicit in the making of our Shitty stories.

Bitch, Please

Now, if you've come this far and still haven't read *A Karmic Introduction*, this would be a good time to take a quick detour. The simplest way to face our own karma is by understanding our own personal karmic theme. But if you're the kind of person who can't move onto something else until you've finished what you've started, or you'd rather not flip-flop between reading material, below is the list of the karmic themes that we lay out in *A Karmic Introduction*.

The way to regard a karmic theme is to imagine your life as a novel or film in which you're the main character. The theme would be the narrative arc of the story through which you, the central character, learn myriad lessons centered around your theme. It often plays out through the relationships we have with others (for example, romantic, family, friends), although it could also be our relationship with a thing (for example, work, career path, missed opportunities). We'll recognize that thing because there will always be a pattern of some kind that is often fraught, stressful, insecure, or unstable. But this pattern which colors our experiences is really only our karmic story. We aren't really unlucky in work, love, money, or life in general. Rather, it is our karmic theme showing us where we can forge our growth and take responsibility for our Shit.

I would be remiss if I didn't mention the other benefit of *A Karmic Introduction*, which is that there are spiritual statements that go with each karmic theme. They are not included here because Rhea said my chapter would be too long… These statements, however, are important because they encompass the meaning and energy of these themes, which can only be fully understood when looking through our spiritual lens. In doing so, as I said before, we gain a wider perspective and are able to see things for what they are—as opposed to what we choose to see to reinforce our chosen narrative.

But of course, since karma just is and does not conform to any ideology, practice, or religion, you do not have to be spiritual to understand or accept its tenets. All it asks is that you see it for what it is because the ability to do that honestly, with an open mind and heart, is how we become powerful.

These are the seven karmic themes (in no particular order for anyone who thinks that shit matters):

1. I Am Unlovable
2 I Am not Worthy
3. I Am Nothing

4. I Am Undeserving
5. I Am Evil
6. I Am Imperfect
7. I Am Broken

It is possible to relate to a few. The reality, however, is that we only have one theme, even if the stories we or others experience have some commonalities. And the more we explore our particular theme, the more we recognize the patterns, choices, and belief systems that underscore how our stories are playing out. What underpins all of them is the core fear that we all hold: *I Am not Good Enough*. This means that even if we cannot pinpoint our specific theme, we can still get to the root of the issue because, beneath all the surface differences that we exhibit, we all carry the same core fear.

Karma gets messy. It also gets difficult and is truly the greatest challenge we face. It takes us to the point of Truth that many of us have been trying to ignore for most of our lives, which is that we really are divine beings having a divine experience in very human way—in contrast to the whole *spiritual-beings-having-a-human-experience* sentiment common in spiritual literature.

That's actually the hallmark of this consciousness game: to remember that we are divine. We do so not to elevate the human experience but to allow the human experience to enrich and teach us because we are doing this in the body for a reason. We came here to fight the good fight, which is to end karma once and for all, to clear the way for future generations to build a better world.

Humans are incredibly talented, creative beings. We are not trying to improve humanity as much as we are trying to free it from the history of enslavement to Separation in which it has been trapped for millennia. While it may be exhausting to be constantly told that children are our future or that we have to work hard for them, the reality is that because we have never sufficiently or efficiently dealt with our karma, we keep foisting it on every other generation to deal with.

As our consciousness grows, we realize there is so much more to being this human being in the body than just sleeping, shitting, fucking, eating, and dying. There's a vast spectrum which includes relating, connecting, communicating, understanding, learning, experiencing, feeling, laughing, and crying—all of which makes being in the body so unique.

The process by which we heal our karma is the process that teaches us how to be empowered in our lives, and that personal empowerment is what we need to truly live our lives as free beings. It's what many of us say we want, but our core fear keeps us trapped into believing it isn't possible. Rhea's story shows that it's not just possible, it's guaranteed.

Rhea's story is not necessarily unique, but it is exceptional, not just because she is an exceptionally talented person but because she got there before many others. Rather than spiritually bypass her Shit, she went dark, lived her life, fell on her ass, and then lived it some more, all the while opening her heart and mind. In doing so, she absorbed all the learning she pushed me to offer as she went through her process.

Rhea generously shares her experiences in this book to help people see that we didn't come here to OM our asses to death to transcend anything and become more spiritual. She shows us that living our lives to the best of our ability, which requires leaning into and burning out our fears, is the way through to a life we could only imagine when we're in our karmic realities.

Karma is merely the beginning of your journey, not the end. And what you are fighting for is your consciousness because consciousness is the only way to true freedom in this world. All you need to do is do four things: trust yourself, have some faith in the process, know that you can do it, and hope for the best.

Love Story
Rhea

It ended in a way that it wasn't supposed to—or so I thought.

In my version of the story, he was what I thought love was supposed to be: the skip in my heart when I saw my phone flash up with his name, the excitement in the moments leading up to seeing him, and the relief when reunited. With him, I had an inexplicable familiarity that felt like coming home, and with every encounter, I plunged further, taking another step that I believed would eventually result in our Happily Ever After.

We had all the ingredients for the perfect love story: how we met, who we were to each other, and the unique bond we shared. The tale fit and I needed the reality to be the same way, so when the cracks started to show, and when the story didn't unfold the way that I thought it should, I rewrote it to help it along. Every action that I could construe as loving from his side (which could be anything from making me dinner to introducing me to his friends) became a reassurance that love was close. Every action that told me otherwise (like taking too long to answer my messages or not sharing his last Rolo) was explained away or course-corrected, and I adjusted my behavior according to the new situation before plowing on.

I was avoiding the big question (do we feel the same way?). To figure that out, I started adding up his feelings in our everyday interactions. Not committing to me properly? No problem. Not telling me he cared? No problem. Not texting me back? Big ass problem. Choosing a movie without taking into consideration my preference? Huge ass problem.

Logic was my compass, evidence was my road map, and the final destination was love. So whenever things deteriorated, I would go into my mind and do everything in my power to rationalize the situation, searching for a different outcome. I sacrificed myself for his happiness, bent my needs so that they fit in with his own, and stage-managed our interactions so he would see how I was perfect for him, just like I believed he was perfect for me.

It didn't matter if it didn't feel right, it didn't matter if I wasn't being treated the way I wanted to be treated, and it definitely didn't matter that being physically next to him sometimes made me feel more alone and unwanted than if I had been by myself. In my story, there was both the possibility of a Happily Ever After and the fear of being alone. I couldn't let the latter win.

But as much as I tried to make it work, this chapter isn't about the Happily Ever After. As much as I thought I loved him (or that there was the potential for more), and as much as our connection existed, it wasn't a partnership in any way. There was no stability, no mutual commitment, and no freedom to be myself.

Every time I swallowed my feelings or turned to him instead of turning towards myself, I reinforced the belief that his feelings mattered to me more than my own. In making excuses for his behavior, justifying my responses, and focusing my world around him, I lost myself. And by allowing everything to be about what he needed and wanted, rather than listening to myself, I wound up settling. I didn't see that I could connect and love someone else who also cared enough to show me in a way that suited me. I believed it was up to me to make the best of our relationship and focus on the good parts (isn't that what the stories tell us to do?), so I thought I had no other choice.

Of course, sometimes I tried to walk away, but at some point, I had to stop the revolving door; not because I wanted to but because the possibility of true love that I had been clinging on to had degraded, and even my mind couldn't make it work anymore. I could no longer tolerate avoiding the truth, manipulating it, or explaining it away.

You Keep Me Hangin' On

The truth is, it wasn't about him. It was all about me. In fact, there wasn't just one *him* at all, and it wasn't only in my romantic relationships, either. It was in every interaction I had with anyone whom I believed mattered to my survival.

There was always a part of me that knew I was settling. But I had taken all the Shit that happened to me over the years (whether it was the family dynamics as a child, the bullshit school drama, or the uncomfortable university experiences) and woven them into a tapestry that illustrated perfectly how I wasn't enough to be loved the way I desired.

I had rewritten a story with love as much harsher, more painful, and less loving than my heart had previously told me it was. Love was found in sacrifice, in service to others, and always earned. Society backed up that story perfectly, as love and happiness were reserved for those who looked and acted a certain way. How much other people loved us was a reflection of how lovable we were.

That was the perspective I took when anything happened to me and the reason for every situation that I experienced. Every person who crossed my path was just another actor in the play of my life. I used them to reinforce the story that love didn't exist for me freely; it was never going to be what I hoped it would be, and it would never last. I introduced a side of myself that I believed others would find attractive, I drove myself mad trying to maintain that carefully constructed façade of indifference and desirability, and I never walked away fast enough because I didn't want to take the risk that I wasn't worth running after. Instead, every time I thought that the relationship was ending, I did something or said something to make it okay again.

When we act a certain way to make someone accept us, we are always going to lose. If it works, then we are stuck wondering if the real us would have ever been enough, because the carefully consructed image of us did the trick instead. And if that doesn't work, then we fall into the trap of believing that if we change, they will change their feelings too. Either way, by not being ourselves, we are left believing that we are not worth loving as we are and never will be.

So here I was, in this terrific situation where I had created this story about myself, but I was so scared of it being true that I was willing to do pretty much anything to avoid it. And every time a potential relationship failed or a connection dissipated, I felt that it should have gone differently. I felt betrayed by my expectations, whilst using the disappointment as more evidence to reinforce the fear that I could never find what I was looking for.

In the last chapter, Liz spoke exhaustively about karma, about the lessons that we have to go through to learn, grow, and evolve into the person we came here to be. It's why the Shit that happens isn't random but perfectly designed for us to become the stronger and freer version of ourselves.

Whether we believe in the universe or nothing, I know now that karma will always apply. Either we are experiencing lesson after lesson to help us see that we are so much more than we are currently giving ourselves credit for, or we are in those situations because we don't believe it could get any better. It doesn't really matter; the relationships and experiences are the same.

Something had to change and running away wasn't going to fix it. Instead, I had to look inward and see how my preconceptions of love were shaping my reality. The bad luck, the disappointments, and the filter that I placed on my experiences were all just reflecting back one simple fact: my life was an expression of who I believed I was and what I believed I was entitled to. Regardless if it was karma, it was definitely my lesson and a lesson that I still hadn't fully learned because the same thing always seemed to happen in my relationships. That meant that I didn't need to just rewrite the story; I had to end it.

I needed to learn the lesson I had ignored and turn the page so that I could start writing a new one. I needed to learn that settling was keeping me from being who I was meant to be. I needed to learn that in prioritizing being loved by someone else, I would remain without it. That was the missing piece. That was what I refer to as my Humongous Lesson.

This story isn't mine anymore. What I had to do to end it, well… more on that in the coming chapters. But I will say this: I had to start at the beginning. I had to face the fear that I was unlovable and challenge it, step by step and piece by piece. I had to acknowledge all the ways in which I'd rejected myself in order to be accepted and take responsibility for how my choices led to my unhappiness.

Nobody's Perfect
Liz

We met at The Evelyn Lounge in New York City's Upper West Side on January 20, 2000. After coming out of university, where there were a variety of ways to engage with people, I was new to adult dating—or what seemed to be how adults dated. After a couple of months of going out and meeting random guys, from creepy stalkers to interested-but-not-really guys, I was over whatever game most singles in Manhattan appeared to be playing. It was going to wreck my soul. I could feel my self-respect slipping through my fingers every time I avoided a phone call from someone I'd given my number to but hadn't really wanted to. I felt lost in the sea of lost souls. So I told the universe, "Enough. I don't want this or anyone." It listened. I wasn't approached or hit on, and I didn't really receive any eye contact for a few months.

Then, the week of January 16, 2000, I woke up and decided I was ready to meet someone. I could feel it was time—not for anyone to be the One but maybe to meet someone who would want to genuinely spend time with me. To have fun. I wasn't seeking a relationship as much as I was seeking companionship, and I was wary of putting any rules or expectations around anything because I'd

35

seen enough during my short time in Manhattan. If I did, I'd be playing the same game everyone else was. So I promised myself three things.

The first was to keep a very open mind. My best friend's dad once told me the person we end up with isn't like the person we would typically date. I'd already experienced the lightning bolt that shattered me into a million pieces. Twice. I didn't need it again. I was determined to get to know a person because I was looking for someone who would be a friend and a lover, not a fan or admirer.

The second thing I promised myself was not to give out my number. (My brothers both told me never to do so, and I quickly learned why.) If I wanted to get to know this person, I needed to be the one to make a little effort and reach out. It wasn't about turning the tables or the thrill of the hunt. Rather, it was about being empowered enough to ensure I was on equal footing with the person, as opposed to playing into someone's power game by waiting for them to call me. I get this doesn't totally apply now because calling isn't the only established form of communication in dating. However, it was about not falling into any kind of communication limbo that would keep me in a holding pattern with the other person. Life is truly too short, and my time was too important to do that.

My third promise to myself was that I would give this person three chances. (I called them strikes because my family loved baseball.) I wasn't going to try to win anyone over or make excuses or listen to anyone else make excuses. My years of dating people from varying cultures and ethnicities taught me a lot about human nature. One of the most common things I learned is that if someone is really interested in being in a relationship, they will make the effort.

Now, before we go further, I have to confess one thing that gave me a leg up in this scenario: I'm psychic. I knew I would meet the man of my life in New York. This came to me as I was driving a U-Haul through Ohio with my best friend and sleeping mother. I also knew I'd meet him through a specific woman because of a series of seemingly random coincidences. I didn't know this when I decided to move to New York on a whim or when I met this woman. I also didn't know when I was going to meet him and how. I figured it could take years (it took six months) and that I'd actually become friends with her (we never saw each other again). Perhaps I could've fished for more information from the universe, but I knew better.

When I met my husband that night, I didn't know he would be my husband. The thing about being psychic or knowing your future is that the more you know, the worse the experience becomes for you, even if it's positive. Expectations are the ultimate killer, whether you know the outcome or not. Rarely is anything delivered in the package or manner we expect, and it would make life boring as hell if that were so. I mean, little surprises me, anyway. Might as well enjoy the moments that do.

When it was time to leave, I let him stumble awkwardly as he asked for my number. Normally, if someone seemed shy, I would preempt their question, but this time I told myself to let him, even though I knew I would turn him down. He had to get through that question because if we were going to get to know each other, he had to learn to be comfortable around me and not expect me to anticipate everything. (For his version of our meeting and first dates, tune into KMB Meets Ricardo.)

After I told him I didn't give out my number, I asked for his. He gave me his business card, which was poor planning on my part when I realized the next day that if I didn't call him at his office, I'd have to wait until Monday. That would've meant I'd have waited three days and seemed like I was following the three-day rule (not sure that's a thing anymore, although I know people still have hang-ups about how much time between texts is appropriate and not seeming too eager). Since I'd declared I wasn't going to play by anyone else's rules other than my own, I called him and we met for a drink that night. Well, I drank a glass of wine, and he spent the entire time on a conference call (an indicator of our future together; didn't have to be psychic to see that). Strike 1.

When I suggested we get together the following evening (had to know if he was going to be worth my time sooner rather than later), he said he couldn't because it was his good friend's girlfriend's birthday. Instead, he suggested dinner that Sunday night. Not being able to squeeze me in for a coffee or drink on a Saturday at any hour? Pushing me off to Sunday? I took it to mean he was uninterested and told myself not to take it personally. After all, I was new to this dating approach. There were plenty of people out there I'd yet to meet. In any case, Strike 2.

That Sunday, we had the worst dinner date at an Italian restaurant that was midway between our apartments (we were already learning to meet halfway). Conversation was painful. He barely spoke, and I couldn't carry the conversation for both of us. When the waiter asked if we wanted dessert, we both declined. I was ready to go home and analyze the date with my roommate, that is, until my date suggested we go for ice cream. Earlier that day, a friend jokingly suggested we do so despite the arctic temperature, so I took it as a sign and said yes. The date looked like it was going to be Strike 3, but fortunately, it turned out to be a foul ball, and we had another chance at bat. We went to Häagen-Dazs, got two pints, went back to my place, and talked for two hours.

Pictures of You

It's unimaginable to think about how people met before the internet and social media. Before, there were the usual avenues: weddings, parties, bars, work, fix-ups, and school. Whatever the options, they were limited compared to today. And, upon meeting, we generally had to take people at face value and trust our instincts, for better or worse. Then dating sites came along and shifted the whole dating landscape.

Today, the world and everyone in it is truly at our fingertips. A quick online search can yield a person's entire personal and professional history and resume. Social media gives us an even broader view of a person's life. Without meeting someone in person, we can "know" almost everything about them. There is nothing blind about a date anymore.

When information is that readily available to us, it removes the many barriers that existed previously. Privacy is virtually non-existent, which means there are little or no secrets anymore. The greater the transparency in our interaction with others, the greater our integrity because we have nothing to hide behind. And the less we have to hide, the more connected we can become. Yet, to be able to connect, we have to be able to move beyond the things that keep us separated from one another. First, it's the fears (that is, the source of our karma) and then our egos.

Our identity is developed around our ego and its informed values. It's what tells us that we're different from (and often better than) others. It holds fast to those qualities—physical, intellectual, and emotional—that we wear as our armor to protect us and make us unassailable to critical eyes. Perhaps it means seeking to be the most attractive in the room, the most intelligent, the wealthiest, the best traveled, or the one who appears to have their act together.

Our egos are the first line of defense to make us seem invulnerable in order to prevent others from spotting our weaknesses. We wear them like masks because we're afraid that others will see what we most fear deep down:

that we're not *good enough*. So we find ways to engage with others based on our ego-defined qualities, leading to a sense of being on the same level with them or in a different league. However this plays out, it keeps us in the loop of that very fear we're actually trying to hide: *I Am not Good Enough*. Unfortunately, the more we engage through our egos, the harder it becomes to see beneath the outer layers and find a person's core—the very essence that truly connects us, where love and compassion reside.

Dating apps are a great example of this, which is ironic given their underlying purpose (or so we're expected to believe) is to connect us to potential love matches. But love doesn't go where it's not welcome, and it cannot navigate beyond the boundaries we erect to protect ourselves.

While we may say that we want love, if we place conditions around what that love is supposed to look like or how it's supposed to arrive in our lives, then whatever we experience will not be actual love but a distorted form of it. So any time we are searching for love or the possibility of it through an app, more often than not, all we end up with is a frustrated attempt to connect our ego with another's.

This doesn't mean that apps can't facilitate an initial meeting. After all, in spite of the seemingly large pool of people that apps have made available to us, the pool really isn't that large, it's merely more accessible. The more we come to know ourselves, our needs, our desires, and our purpose, the smaller that pool becomes, until it leaves a mere handful. After that, it takes discernment to be able to find our match.

Developing discernment doesn't just mean knowing ourselves; discernment also tells us how that self fits in with the world around us as well as our relationship with it and others. Discernment is that inner guide, that bullshit barometer that's willing to call us out when we're not acting authentically and tells us to walk away from someone who isn't being authentic with us.

The more discernment we show when we swipe or choose a potential partner, the stronger it gets. But it isn't easy to exercise discernment when we're using these apps. Our truth can go right out the window when we see that someone has the perfect height, an amazing career, a fuckable face, beautiful eyes, or a gorgeous smile. We've traded so many of our real heart's desires for fantasy that we've lost the inner guidance that knows how to spot someone who might just fit us perfectly, even if they don't fit our idealized list.

Our egos love the ideal. They love the idea of perfection. They love the notion that somewhere out there is someone who will make us feel complete. But egos aren't complete. They're the surface layer we've formed to protect us from the world. So we seek out the seemingly flawless person to reflect back to us our ego projection, to assure us that we're as wonderful as we need to believe we are.

As long as we continually connect to others via our ego, we will remain in its power, determining whether someone is either too good or not *good enough* based on arbitrary criteria that don't speak to the soul of the person or their life experiences or have anything to do with who they really are. Instead, we swipe and move on.

The potential of that person cannot be determined if we're locked in our own ego state that wants and needs validation, stemming from the insecurities we haven't yet healed. But the ego keeps us on a short leash. As an outward projection of our karma, it's always reminding us we're unlovable, not worthy, nothing, undeserving, evil, imperfect, or broken to belong in a healthy relationship that demands respect, equality, love, and compassion.

The more we live from our ego, the more likely we are to attract someone who does the same. The ego has an insatiable appetite, so it wants us to keep swiping to make sure the trough stays full. And the more our egos love being fed with attention, validation, and admiration, the less likely we are to heal the issues that gave rise to that ego. The only way to move beyond the ego when it comes to swiping right and first meetings is to ask ourselves, "What am I getting from this interaction?"

It isn't about how the other person makes us feel about ourselves but how we feel in their presence. Contrary to what romance stories or popular dating sites tell us, it isn't about the other person making us feel attractive, smart, sexy, or competent (that's just what the ego wants). Rather, it's about feeling comfortable, honest, and vulnerable so that we can be open and reveal our most authentic selves. This means not having to sell ourselves to the person across from us as if we're interviewing for a relationship.

To operate from our most authentic selves, it takes unloading some of the baggage that keeps us from being open. It takes confronting our karma over and over again until there's nothing left to separate us from ourselves.

Call Me Maybe
Rhea

A few weeks after my Humongous Lesson ended, I downloaded a dating app because I thought the perfect way to feel better was to be reminded that I was still attractive to the opposite sex. But I hadn't given myself any time to process the lesson, and someone else's attention couldn't help me do that. So, in trying to show myself that I was still a catch, I ended up reminding myself of how broken I already felt and how little I wanted to acknowledge it.

I pretended to family and friends the reason I didn't want to date was because I wanted to heal and get over it so that I wouldn't tarnish the new relationship with the old. But the truth was, I just wasn't ready to put myself out there and run the risk of getting told I wasn't *good enough* again. So I waited and watched everyone else instead—for a long time. Like a classic Richard Curtis montage, I watched friends go on their first dates, go on subsequent ones, move in together, celebrate their first anniversaries, get engaged, get married, and have children (not necessarily in that order and some missed a few steps along the way).

Every now and again, another happily coupled-up friend would tell me a story about how the girl down the road was shacking up with some dude she met on the internet. So I would download, swipe a couple of times, and reconfirm that I wasn't ready. I was curious, but all it took was a quick foray into the dating world before I scuttled back off again.

In one of these dipping-my-toes-back-into-the-dating-pool experiments, I met someone, and we seemed to click. But then we got a bit too close and a bit too real (we hadn't even met yet, but my threshold for both of those things was very low at the time), so I bolted. I used the same excuses that I'd been using for a while when I justified not being on the apps: there was no point getting attached because I couldn't guarantee that it would be worth it.

After a few unanswered texts over the next couple of months, where he tried to figure out what went wrong, he gave up. I know, not cool, but I wasn't ready to be honest, or even ready to lie.

A couple of years later, and after another my-friend-from-work-went-on-Tinder-and-met-her-husband-and-you-should-try-it speech, I decided it was finally time to take the apps more seriously. Not too seriously mind you, my goal was simple: feel attractive again after feeling very meh.

The first step was to choose some good pictures (the hardest part). Obviously, they had to be flattering but not so flattering that I didn't look like me. I had to include a variety of different poses and backgrounds. And I obviously couldn't upload one that looked like a selfie—I needed to show that I didn't need to take pictures of myself and had friends who could do that for me instead.

The second step was to answer the questions. I chose them carefully, had a cigarette whilst thinking about the answers (obviously I didn't admit I smoked publicly; it doesn't make anyone cool anymore), and declared that I listened to questionable music and that I couldn't ride a bike. Now I was ready to start swiping.

What. An. Ego. Boost.

Here, unlike in real life, people were telling other people that they found them attractive, all with a flick of a thumb. When I swiped on a cute guy and they swiped back to make a match, I felt validated and wanted more. Behind the protection of a small screen, I became a swiping addict, totally forgetting that these were actual people. Dating became a numbers game, and the prize wasn't a partner, it was as many objectively hot matches as I could get.

I started juggling conversations, forgetting who was where and what they wanted, forgetting whom I liked and whom I was chatting to just for the sake of the chat (and because I felt bad saying no). I would get lost in the idea of the tall ones, the cute ones, the dangerous ones, and the *very* flirty ones. Those who would have possibly been better partners got lost in the mess.

But every now and again, someone would bridge the gap between the app and reality and ask to meet up. That's when I would freak out.

The image I had curated online was a very deliber-ate one. It included the aspects I wanted them to see and hid the ones I didn't. It was a façade of my personality and a mirage of my looks. Yes, I could have put up some pictures where I looked bad, and I could have opened up my heart to everyone who crossed my phone, but that wouldn't have gotten me anywhere. I liked the attention, and this version of me was getting it.

But all it was actually doing was causing me to further doubt myself. For every person who liked me, there was always the question of whether they would like me if they saw me or spoke to me. For every person who told me that I was beautiful, I wondered if they would feel the same way when sitting next to me. For every person who told me I was funny or sexy, I was scared that they wouldn't feel that way in real life.

Those chasms got bigger as I met the people on the other side of the internet. An overzealous online search may tell us everything we need to know about someone's job, but it can't tell us if they are kind, if they are patient, or if they have more or fewer hang-ups than we do. There were men who wanted to pretend they were better than internet dating (you know, the ones who profess that they will lie about meeting online), there were men who were at least a foot shorter than their pictures or just didn't look like them at all, and there were men who were sweet towards me yet rude with everyone else. (Side note: no one seems to eat on these dates, only drink; so for a variety of reasons, we're even pretending that we don't need food to survive.)

Every first date came with a side order of a crushing reality check. So much so that some wouldn't even make it to the first date at all, either turning into weird sexy pen pals or weird boring pen pals where we just periodically exchanged random pieces of information about how our day went. Some got too relationship-y before we'd even seen each other, and some, after warming you up with normal conversation, would change up the vibe without any indication or solicitation that it was appropriate to do so… and send the one thing most women don't understand (or are offended by) but men think we can't stop desiring: the dick pic.

Get Lucky

I was looking for the most personal thing in the most impersonal way. And it wasn't working for me. Yes, I had some great stories; but because I wanted to meet someone, or at least connect in some way, these guys were just disappointing me with the impersonal nature of dating.

I couldn't tell who would suit me from the showcase of pictures and comments that were designed to illustrate one side of me yet hide all the parts that were actually fundamental in partnering up. I also couldn't see who was serious about meeting or who would disappear for no reason halfway through a sentence, never to return. And I couldn't connect to them either because I was doing the same. I was scared when someone tried to make it personal: when they wanted to chat on the phone instead of exchanging endless vapid messages, when they actually wanted to get to know me, when they said they were interested and meant it.

And when there was a chance for connection, I followed the old rules of dating anyway, ensuring that we weren't connecting but just playing out the gendered roles dictated to us by society.

But I still swiped. What else was I meant to do?

Every now and again, the guy I ghosted all those years ago would cross my mind. The shame that I ended up being one of those people who just disappeared without explanation would creep back in. But I didn't think there was much I could do about it, apart from learning from my mistakes, so I resolved that going forward I would never do it again.

Four years after I left him hanging, whilst searching for an address on my phone, an old text of his came up. With new experiences and perspectives under my belt, I was a bit more open than I was when we first interacted, so I messaged him to apologize. I knew most would have just left it alone, but I couldn't, not now I had been confronted with it and there was something I could do. Luckily, he replied. "Hey, you. I remember you. Yes, life got in the way. Lovely, nothing really to be sorry for, it happens to the best of us. I am single… Drink next weekend?"

Imagine that. Instead of telling me where to go, he shrugged off his ego and just took my apology in his stride.

But since my last foray logging on to the apps, I was better at playing the game, only choosing those who were exactly right on paper and framing myself as the same. He wasn't the type in my head that I thought would work, not because he wasn't a great guy but because I had decided exactly who my partner would be, and he didn't tick every box. But how could I say no? I couldn't. I had literally just apologized for not giving him a chance. I couldn't just do it again. So I went.

What followed was one of the best dates I had ever been on. I explained what happened to me and why I didn't respond the first time. He explained the relationship he had just been in and how that hadn't ended very well. Our start, and the fact we hadn't spoken online for years, meant that all those barriers, those that are usually up when we interrogate someone for the role of potential mate, were gone. As a result, not only was it comfortable, but it was also fun.

We didn't last, but that was for none of the reasons that I listed the first time he came into my life. Even our ending was another easy lesson. We said goodbye in a way that recognized our attraction and the romance of our reconnection with both mutual respect and honesty. As a result, I learned what it meant to own a feeling, say it with pride, and hear the other person do the same.

Could it get better than that? There was nothing disappointing about this person whom I had written off before we started, and I can say that a lot of the dating experiences that went well after him were, in part, thanks to the moment I sent that message apologizing. Don't get me wrong; some of the experiences to come didn't go well at all. But that was because I still had other things left to learn.

Heartbreaker
Liz

There's always one person at the center of an integral lesson. For some, it's a parent or family member, for others, it's a close friend, but for many, it's a lover. No matter the nature of the relationship, what needs to exist at the core of that relationship is some kind of love, because the more love we experience, the more invested we are in the relationship.

Every relationship, every single one we have in this lifetime, is intended to teach us something. That does not mean it's meant to disappoint us or that it's transient. Rather, any time we're experiencing or feeling love, that emotion is meant to take us deeper into ourselves and allow us to tap into our greater wisdom. That wisdom comes when we have our hearts broken, because the more our hearts are broken, the more open they become. And the more open they are, the more we are able to heal those fears that keep us imprisoned in lives we don't enjoy.

We asked for this. Relationships (technically contracts among souls) ensure that we are getting the lessons we want in this lifetime. But it's our limited understanding of love that confuses us. When we feel love, we often believe the relationship isn't supposed to end. So we put more effort into staying together and keeping the peace than we do in understanding the lesson. And it's the same lesson every time.

We are whole.

That is, beneath the layers of our karma, and beneath our thin layer of ego, lies a complete and whole person worthy of the greatest love possible. But that love is enabled when we've been broken open. This is only possible when we've reached the depths of our hearts that reveal that somewhere, at some point in our lives, we knew we were enough.

It often takes more than one person to bring us to the lesson. Perhaps there was one who pierced our hearts, but our resilience or stubbornness propelled us forward. When that happens, we may think we're finished with the lesson. Spoiler alert: we never are. There are always layers to the lesson, and the greater our consciousness, the more enriched our wisdom becomes. So maybe a second person entered our lives and shook us up, allowing the fears we thought we'd successfully buried beneath the surface to emerge so that we had to confront them. But nothing compares to the moment when our hearts are cracked open enough and we are jolted awake by some cosmic force of love that tells us that this is going to be one hell of a lesson. This is where Dave enters the picture.

Everyone has a Dave. Everyone. Dave isn't the lesson. Dave isn't even the love. Dave is the connector between us and our pain. And whatever and however Dave arrives, the experience or lesson is rarely what we expect.

Daves are everywhere at the moment. Because we are at such a pivotal time in our evolutionary history as spiritual beings, we need the Daves to open us up. Without a Dave, it would be nearly impossible to divest ourselves from our karma and egos and develop some semblance of inner peace. It's inner peace that will move us into love, and Dave will do exactly what is necessary to get us there. And what is one of the moves Dave uses to break our hearts? Ghosting.

Ghosting is a breakdown in communication. It's one of the greatest scourges to arise out of this era of dating. Contrary to the many theories out there as to why it's happening or the issues surrounding it (generally, it's a lack of courage, fear of vulnerability, or an indication of how insensitive people have become), it has everything to do with our lack of discernment.

It's understandable. Love is blind, after all. Except it isn't. We are the ones who are blind. We are the ones who diminish ourselves in order to fit into relationships. We are the ones who refuse to act when we spot the red flags a mile away. We are the ones who make excuses, who justify, who reason, who create stories to make us feel like we belong with someone when we really don't. We are the ones who fear communicating our needs and desires because we think that person won't want us anymore. And when we experience fear in a relationship, it's because we're not facing our own fears—fears that have nothing to do with the other person.

Being ghosted is a shock to our system. It wakes us from the somnolence of our comfort zone that has taught us to believe what we're experiencing is enough. We have checklists that assure us everything is okay so long as our fantasy life, or the one we think we're supposed to be leading, appears great on the surface. Yet, what we're neglecting to do at every disappointing turn is to look inside and ask ourselves, "Where am I not enough?"

Just as the lesson is always "Where am I not enough?", the answer is always "When I cannot be myself." In other words, it's when I cannot step outside of my ego to connect to myself.

Daves are literal food for the soul. Dave brings us back to our karma. Every. Single. Time. Unlovable, not worthy, nothing, undeserving, evil, imperfect, and broken. The experience of being ghosted, losing love, or being abandoned points to that fundamental issue of *I Am not Good Enough*. When we reach our pain, we can finally acknowledge it was always there, long before Dave entered the picture. We just never had context for it before.

This is why we can't ever completely blame any one person for our pain. Our hurts are the results of a series of decisions made by us for our growth, to enable us to heal and evolve. The upside to Dave is that once we've come far enough in our healing, any significance attributed to Dave dissipates—whether he's the love of our lives, the best sex we've ever had, the most sensitive person we've ever known, or the one who most influenced us. And as soon as we've integrated the lesson that we are whole beings, Dave's story ends and ours begins. For many of us, that's a story yet to be written.

Hotline Bling
Rhea

Starting to date again was exciting. The more I was validated, the more my confidence grew, and I stopped feeling romantically impotent. But I didn't quite know who I was, what product I was selling, or even what a healthy relationship looked like. So whatever stage of the dating process I was in, and whomever I was in it with, I was interviewing for a job that I had convinced myself was needed. Sure, I was assessing the person in front of me to see whether they would fit me, but more importantly, I was trying to make sure that I would fit them. It wasn't real, and it wasn't connecting. It was our egos playing a game of chicken.

An unfortunate side effect of not knowing who I was, nor having the courage to admit what I wanted, was using my friend's experiences as a barometer for what I should accept. I started seeing my dates through their eyes, the funny or romantic stories I would tell when I got home, the dramatic twists for their enjoyment, and the screenshots of the text messages to evidence it all. But when my dates acted in a way I believed my friends would deem unacceptable, I made excuses or just rewrote the interaction entirely for my benefit and theirs. I told myself that I wasn't taking it too seriously anyway and that it was more of a rebranding exercise than anything else.

That was until I met my Dave.

When I first met him, we clicked immediately. In long conversations, where my hands would cramp from typing on my phone for hours on end, it felt as though we had both found what we had been looking for (which is quite interesting considering I am not sure either of us even knew what that was). All my learned tactics to present my best self were working, and all his learned tactics to do the same were hitting the mark too. I hid the parts of myself that I didn't think he would like, and he threw little white lies around like confetti so that I wouldn't see who he really was. The result was that we got on GREAT. In every conversation we had, every laugh we shared, and every compliment received, I opened my heart a little bit more.

Instead of looking at our gaping incompatibilities as a problem, I merely saw them as obstacles that could be overcome. A part of me knew that he wasn't actually the person I had decided that he was (and he definitely wasn't acting like it), but my heart was already opening, so I stayed the course. Our connection, and the potential of a future, allowed me to ignore the reality of the present.

I became mired in the excuses I had created for his behavior, and instead of just accepting that this wasn't right and walking away, I simply lowered my expectations of him to make it fit. I suggested seeing each other casually rather than seriously (to mitigate the differences between us, thereby keeping him in my life without having to explain why I was doing so to myself and others). We had long periods of silence and no trust, and even though I wanted a partnership, I kept dating other people because what he was giving me wasn't enough.

But in handing him every excuse in the book, I moved further and further away from who I was and what I wanted—all because I had found someone who clicked enough with me that I could settle for. But the problem was, the more I settled, the more I was asked to settle even further. I wanted more from his seduction routine than a 2 a.m. "r u up" text, but because I had become so convincing in my apparent lack of care towards him, I pretended it was enough. I wanted to be chosen, and I wanted to be loved, but the reasons why I wanted that love were actually the reasons preventing me from finding it.

We come into the world knowing that we are whole and perfect, but as we get older, the people and the experiences around us teach us otherwise. We start to believe that there is something wrong with us, whether that's our personality, status, intelligence, looks, or lifestyle. They are things that lead us to ridicule or be ridiculed, or things that we believe make us unattractive to others. They are what stop us from being open, trusting, and ready to give and receive love. Simply put, our mind tells us that they are the attributes that stand between us and unconditional love.

Whatever they are (and they are different for everyone), they are the parts that we have spent the majority of our lives either pretending don't exist or trying to hide. They are our shadows. And we have been trying so hard to hide them from others to avoid rejection, that we usually have also hidden them from ourselves.

Of course we have. Rejection hurts, whichever way it comes, whatever precedes it, and regardless of what follows. It can hurt far more than the person who is rejecting us warrants, not because of the act itself but because of what the act represents. It confirms our deepest fears that we haven't hidden enough of who we really are. So when we are rejected, however we are rejected, we will always blame the reasons that we have already decided do not make us *good enough*, anyway.

Those aspects I banished were part of who I was, and they were never reasons why someone couldn't love me. My mind had decided that in order to contextualize my pain and had weaved a story to seemingly protect me from it happening again. Dave showed me perfectly how I would do anything in my power to avoid being abandoned by someone else—all because I was scared. Instead of admitting what I really wanted (a relationship) with whom I wanted (someone who fit me), I was settling for an imitation instead. I wasn't asking the real questions: if I could believe for a moment that I was perfect as I was, would I want our interaction to continue like this? Of course not.

Ouch. The only thing stopping me from getting what I really wanted was believing I was enough and using that faith in myself to get it. Even if that faith was misplaced (by the way, it never is), getting what I really wanted could only be possible if I gave myself the chance to find out.

And that's where I realized it needed to start, with me turning up as myself (yes, with room for improvement, as always, but not as a hologram of what I thought was acceptable) and looking for my own partner, rather than trying to contort myself enough to be someone else's ideal instead. Because the more I rejected myself, the more the other person would reject me; the more I failed to love who I was, the more I ensured that others would not love me too; the more I presented myself as someone's fantasy, the more I couldn't find my own.

I needed to remember the times when I was chosen and the times I didn't want to be; because no matter how we spin it, just as we have been rejected at points, we have rejected others too.

Dave may have sucked, but he was a gift that kept on giving. He was the person who allowed me to see the dark parts of myself that I had been hiding and see they were never dark at all. He was never a bad guy or the wrong guy, but he wasn't my right guy, either. He was just the right guy for the job. In consistently lowering his effort with me, he showed me that settling for less meant that I would be treated as less. In consistently choosing him over myself, he pushed me low enough to see that there was only one choice left: to allow the walls that I had built between the different parts of myself (the walls that told me that he was enough and I wasn't) to crumble, leaving a different space instead—the space to be me.

Unbreak My Heart
Rhea

After being exposed to the undeniable fact that my wounds were dictating how I acted and reacted to romantic stimuli, it was clear that for anything to change, I had to tend to them rather than ignore them. I hadn't been taking responsibility for the pain and understanding my part in a situation and learning from it (healthy), I had been surrendering to the belief that I wasn't *good enough* and allowing that belief to become the certainty of my past, my present, and my future (unhealthy). If I wanted out of my Shit, I needed out of the definition I had created about myself too.

Something needed to change, and it was time to put my mind to work for me rather than against me. Through extensive journaling, talking, meditating, and listening (to others and myself), I discovered that a lot of the evidence I had gathered, that led me to believe I wasn't *good enough*, was not evidence at all. A lot of it was just my way of trying to remain in control. If I could blame myself for getting hurt, that meant that it was less likely to happen again.

My warped account of history didn't explain my experiences, and it definitely didn't define who I was. I fixated on the experiences that backed up the belief that I was not *good enough* and conveniently forgot the ones that challenged it. As hard as it was to see, for every event that I internalized that told me I was unlucky in love, I ignored others that showed the opposite. For every object of my affection who didn't choose me, there was another who did. For every piece of me that someone told me wasn't attractive, I found many who said otherwise. Turns out, I was basing the value of my relationships and experiences on the outcome and my insecurities, rather than seeing them for what they were.

I deduced a new pattern: all the incidents that caused me to believe I needed fixing were usually a reaction to someone else's issues. It was like a contagious disease: we were infecting each other with pain, leaving deep scars that we would then carry into the next experience, only to infect someone else when we refused to acknowledge that they were there. Maybe we felt so insecure that we ended a relationship before it began, leaving the other person confused as to what they did wrong (when in reality it had nothing to do with them at all). Maybe the other person then walks into the next relationship scared that they are going to get hurt again, only to then infuse that relationship with dishonesty and control. No matter where the initial hurt came from, by not dealing with it, we are perfectly poised to push it onto the next relationship we have, ensuring that not only is it what we experience again but that the other person experiences it too.

The ego may lead us to believe that there is nothing wrong with us because it wants to keep us safe from facing our core fear, but without facing our fears, we end up projecting them onto others and exacerbating them instead. We blame others for our issues, we pretend we don't blame ourselves, or we do just enough to superficially excuse them, without ever taking full responsibility. Either way, unless we truly own them, they don't go away, and we end up looping through and spreading around our Shit, wondering why nothing ever truly gets better.

As a result, I developed a different theory: if we could spread the pain by connecting to others, then surely we could also spread the antidote. So I started dating with that intention in mind: to heal through connection rather than to continue letting it hurt me. That meant this time I wasn't looking for the One, I was simply looking to learn something better.

I didn't want to get hurt, though; that would defeat the purpose. So whilst I wanted to play nice with others, I also needed to make sure that they would also play nice with me. How I could ensure that? By avoiding making it about emotional investment because that would leave me exposed.

But looking for a connection, whilst also not wanting to feel within that connection, is an interesting exercise in contradiction… I may have wanted not to get hurt, but in avoiding feeling the "icky" emotions, I was also ensuring that I would miss out on the other (nicer) ones. It was definitely a misguided Adventure in Connecting.

Double-edged relationships were becoming my thing. First, there was the Italian. I knew pretty quickly that there was no spark for me. But that was okay; sparks weren't safe, and they were to be avoided during the experiment, anyway. And it seemed to be working. I woke up every morning with a message telling me how beautiful I was, got sent random pictures when I was bored, and never worried that a reply wasn't coming my way.

I had the security I needed and the compliments I craved. But although we had the physical connection of teenagers, my heart didn't sing when his name flashed up on my phone, my tummy didn't flutter when I saw him, and when I was next to him, he never commanded my full attention—and I knew he felt the same.

Whilst our conversation was peppered with poetry, it wasn't real and we were never committed to each other in any way (except that we were both noncommittal). We were there to make the other feel less lonely. He never did anything to hurt me or make me cry, and I never felt like I was less than. But I also never felt alive.

Yes, I felt desired, beautiful, sexy, and oftentimes impenetrable. But that is nowhere near as great as we think it's going to be. That isn't a connection at all; it's just two people existing alongside each other, both too scared to be hurt but not scared enough to stay out of the game entirely. I wanted to be shown that I was lovable, but without the actual connection to underpin it, it meant far less than it should have and made the experience of having someone say all the right things far less special.

Stuck In The Middle With You

Then there was the other one. And oh, did we have fireworks. Our first interactions laid the groundwork for what was poised to become the perfect situation. We seemed to be massively drawn in by each other, but we both didn't want the emotional requirement that came with a relationship. Just like the ones who made an impact before him, the initial interactions between us were electrified with constant talking, sharing, and mutual admiration. There was one difference, however: we both had made it clear that this wasn't going to be a forever thing. He made it about physical needs, I made it about consistent validation, and we both made it transient.

Still, we were infatuated and addicted from the start. Urgent messaging followed by welcomed over-familiarity; we arranged our first date three hours after we started chatting. Three days later, I was excited, nervous, and ready to cancel—not because I didn't want to go but because I didn't want to lose the high just yet.

Then it got even better. Within moments of being together, we settled into this intense attraction, where his gentle caressing, something that would have been too forward in the past, sparked my anticipation of what was to come. Our first kiss, an hour in, didn't feel like the first and left me craving more. Infatuated, and with the zeal of an addict looking for their next hit, my world was narrowed down to one person. Except in my desire to not care, I betrayed myself in a far more fundamental way, by ignoring every red flag in the book.

Red flags being ignored again… This seemed to be the only pattern I was still consistent with—which makes sense. Regardless of all the work I had done, I was still approaching him from a place of fear because I needed proof that my stories were mistaken, and getting hurt would have reinforced my fear rather than alleviated it.

We also had chemistry, and I enjoyed spending time with him, whether or not he was the One. I couldn't not care about him; we were connecting on some level. But in making such a concerted effort to remove any *intimacy* from our interactions, all we were actually doing was removing the *integrity* from our interactions instead.

We both put up our own boundaries to separate us from our feelings. We called it a fling, we joked about it being transactional, he tried to second-guess my emotions, and I tried to put arbitrary conditions into our relationship. In fact, there were many rules to control the relationship: no phone calls, what pictures could be sent, and no public displays of affection (a quick iPhone search of the word *rules* pulls up at least twenty-seven mentions from just our conversations). But we also broke nearly every single one, and our interactions had even less integrity than they did before.

What a mess. Even I could see that, and I was in it. My mind may have gotten its new evidence, and my story may have changed, but denying emotions was fucking it up for everyone.

What was meant to be simple became complicated. That is what emotions and pressure do. When we tried to remove both, we ended up doing the opposite. He started feeling things that were never my intention; and I started feeling everything. Oh, and the punchline? Even though this dance had continued for a couple of months, it never really progressed to anything other than some meaningful eye gazes in that time.

I may have wanted a different experience, but in approaching this interaction from a place of protection, and in refusing to acknowledge that there was a possibility that my feelings could grow, I sealed our fate. It wasn't about figuring out who I was. I always knew that deep down. It was about accepting what I wanted and not cheating my way into love by bypassing the scary stuff.

When my mind was running the show, it was bending itself to the will of my fears and ego; it was all about protection, with no faith in any kind of love. It was all about hedging and attempting to avoid potential hurt. But I couldn't connect to anything if I wasn't even connected to my own heart. So in order for me to experience anything truly different, I had to approach it differently too. And whilst that could involve getting hurt, I decided it would be worth it because with the scary stuff comes the real payoff.

To truly connect to someone else, we must be connected to ourselves. I didn't want a relationship that was all smoke and mirrors, and I definitely didn't want to keep playing in my fears whilst hoping they would miraculously disappear. But in controlling my relationships to avoid (unsuccessfully, I might add) a fallout, I was ensuring it. My mind had been doing the best it could, but without connecting to my heart, I was never going to experience what I wanted. That meant I had to deal with the emotions that I had been avoiding, rather than explaining them away with logic. It was time to Go Dark.

Everybody Hurts
Liz

If we're going to be the greatest version of ourselves, without the weight of our karma bearing down on us, then we have to Go Dark. To do this means to go within and wrestle with our story: *How Am I not Good Enough?* Unlovable? Not Worthy? Undeserving? Nothing? Imperfect? Evil? Broken? We all have the answer.

Each of our relationships and experiences points to it. But many of us have spent a good portion of our lifetimes hiding from our karma, so it takes uncovering the story layer by layer, perhaps one relationship or mishap at a time, until we can finally reach the core of the story without self-destructing.

Even though we can begin with an intellectual awareness of our issue, we need to be able to reach the emotional level to truly heal it. This is where it gets rocky. Our emotional range has been limited. Society has made it so. In order to fit into our family and social units, it's been ingrained in us to be good, kind, sincere, giving, and virtuous. If we don't live up to those standards, we're deemed bad, wrong, selfish, and immoral. Shame is the tool that keeps us in line because it reinforces the belief that we're not *good enough* so we keep trying to prove otherwise. Thus, we remain in a karmic loop.

The longer we remain in the karmic loop, the more tired we are; and the more exhausted we become, the more inclined we are to give up and believe we are all of those things we know we are not: unlovable, not worthy, nothing, undeserving, evil, imperfect, or broken. To reinforce this message, we create a filter that only allows us to see our stories in a way that perpetuates this negative self-image.

We can try to fight it. There are the Pollyannas of the world who refuse to see reality for what it is. They may recite daily affirmations, read self-help books, and watch inspiring stories about others overcoming seemingly insurmountable odds. But hope doesn't stand a chance because meaningful change begins with acknowledging the pain within rather than passing it through the positivity filter. Then there are the cynics who refuse to see reality for what it could be. While it helps to see things as they are, without the idea that things can be better, this leaves little room for improvement. Either way, the results wind up the same.

To Go Dark isn't meant to hurt us any more than we've already been hurt. It isn't meant to take us to the brink of self-harm either (which is an externalization of our pain). It's meant to bring us to our pain which we've kept locked inside, beneath the ego, that has played out in the form of our karma—from the hurt we experienced when we've felt judged, ridiculed, or unsafe, to the acute pain that we feel from living and being in body every day. It's the kind of pain we desperately avoid by numbing it with every kind of substance imaginable. It's the pain of merely existing in a world of Separation and polarity.

Life hurts. From the moment we enter this world, it hurts. Our wants and our daily needs, from the physical to the emotional, are bound up in discomfort. The distractions we seek are often in response to the myriad pains we feel. We spend so much of our lives (and money) figuring out how to best meet our needs—and mitigate the pain—that all too often we don't have the time or the wherewithal to transcend our physical existence and grow into our spiritual selves, which is where true healing takes place. To do this, we need to move past the pursuit of pleasure (which we often mistake for the pursuit of happiness) or numbing, which keeps us separated from our pain.

Moving past the pursuit of pleasure isn't easy because there's so much about life that keeps us distracted—dating apps, social media, the day-to-day grind, raising children, supporting spouses, careers, and family needs. There's no end to the busyness of our lives. But there comes a time when we all hit a wall or receive that wake-up call to the thing we've been avoiding for most of our lives—the hurt or the pain that we've been carrying inside. And because it's on the inside, we have no choice but to go within to discover what it is and its source.

We go inside by asking ourselves, "When am I most in pain?" We all have triggers. Perhaps someone didn't follow through on a promise to text or meet up, and it drives us into a spiral of feeling abandoned. Perhaps we got an unflattering haircut or someone criticized our look, sending us into depression because we fear no one will ever find us desirable. Perhaps our cohorts are being recognized or promoted at work while we find ourselves stagnating and questioning our life choices. Perhaps we're on the receiving end of infidelity or a friendship betrayal. Or perhaps no one particular thing has happened, but we're acutely aware that somehow, somewhere, our lives went off track.

In isolation, some of these examples may not seem particularly life-changing or enough to make us question our existence. However, the reality is that it doesn't take much to push us over the precipice that many of us hover over daily. Many of us are so used to taking up residence on the edge that we think it's normal, all while pretending we're not on the brink to make it all seem okay. There are four ways in which our pain manifests itself spiritually.

1. If I am not loved, how will I love?

Love isn't a transitive property. It begins and ends with us every time. If it's seen as limited, then our experience of it will be limited. Love eludes us when we don't source it from within first. So in asking ourselves this question, we forget that we cannot look outside ourselves for validation.

At its core, we must first recognize that we are Love and that the source is an unlimited reservoir. It takes some digging to get there—digging through old patterns, stories, disappointments, and hurts. And so we have to go through each story, one by one, until we've reached the source that reminds us *I Am Love*.

2. If I am not living my purpose, what is the point of my life?

What is the point of our existence? It's not the pursuit of happiness or even love. It's to come into our divinity (which is ultimately the source of our power). It's easy to believe love is what it's all about because love is more than just an emotion or experience. It's the portal through which we come into our divinity. Love transcends everything from pain to pleasure, from hurt to happiness. Love can move us through the entire emotional spectrum and bring us to our spiritual selves.

With that said, if we think love is enough, then we fall short of our ultimate goal. And it's okay if we do. It doesn't mean we're failing at life. But if we wish to discover something more during our brief time in this human experience, then it's important to push through our understanding, open our minds to all that we cannot see, and throw trust, faith, and hope into the air and see where they all land—to not be afraid of embracing our greatest desires and live our lives fully.

To make something our purpose, we must embody it, love the idea of it, love the idea of engaging with it, and move through it with unwavering commitment. It may not be our day jobs that we use to keep a roof over our heads; it may not be the second job we use to feed ourselves or our families; it may not even be something that we can commodify that brings us financial abundance; but our purpose will always, one hundred percent, ultimately propel us forward and bring us joy, even if it isn't easy. And it's something we don't have to do alone. However, it's important not to confuse shared purpose with someone being our purpose, whether it be a lover or even our children. Our purpose does not rest with another person (more on this in Chapter Twenty-Five).

3. If I am not God, then who am I?

At the core of our entire being is God, which is the core of Oneness consciousness. (If you want more information, refer to our podcasts; for example, Lost Stars, Find Your Love, Hard Knock Life, or any other episode from seasons 1–5). Whether we believe in any god has nothing to do with Oneness consciousness, which involves acknowledging that at our core *is* God. The former puts God outside of ourselves as a kind of being that grants wishes, favors, answers prayers, blesses, invokes fires and floods, is omnipotent, and influences our very existence. The latter acknowledges that we are all connected by a source of creation, and that very source is us. We are our creator.

Our inability or unwillingness to acknowledge this has everything to do with Separation, which we call *trauma*. If I and God are not One, then our sense of self and identity is null and void. If we are in Separation, or our trauma causes us to remain in Separation, our darkest place has everything to do with that identity crisis. The way through is Oneness, that is, integrating the Divine self by acknowledging *I Am God*.

4. If I am not me, how will I have peace?

We are taught to conform at a young age. Values are instilled in order to distinguish right from wrong. Socially acceptable behaviors are modeled by those close to us, and we're disciplined with rules and consequences at both home and school. We're always being groomed to be "model citizens."

All the ways that help us survive our world of polarity and Separation hurt us when we come into Oneness consciousness because they are not in integrity. To be able to be whole and at One means we cannot engage in behaviors that separate us from ourselves and others. It creates a dissonance so great (and which is becoming greater with every generation) that we are forced to choose; otherwise, we face our own self-destruction. The harder the old guard pushes to stifle the youth, the louder they become. And the message is clear: it is time, just as it's always been, to come fully into our *be*-ing. It's the only way to live our purpose.

We cannot live our purpose if we hold judgment. More likely than not, we've judged others (even our friends) for being "soft" or "too sensitive" if they couldn't handle what we may deem as one of life's many disappointments. Yet we can't possibly know another person's pain or how much they've experienced in their lifetime. When we judge others, we're merely reinforcing the shame we once experienced. And the more we judge and shame others, the more we reside in our karmic loop. What we're really doing is refusing to acknowledge our own trauma, and it takes healing our own wounds to show others compassion.

The way to peace with-out is to have peace within. The only way to have peace within is to bring ourselves into wholeness. The only way to bring ourselves into wholeness is to be ourselves completely, unwaveringly, fearlessly, and without shame or judgment. Because at our core, we are One. We are all connected. And by being connected, our existence isn't challenged or threatened by anyone else. It's Separation that teaches us that our survival means we have to change, shift, or contort ourselves to fit in. The reality is that by being ourselves, we will fit even better than before because we all exist within the infinite space of Love.

It's in that space where we can declare *I Am Me*.

Courage to Change
Rhea

When it came to understanding the Shit that had happened to me, it became clear that my mind could only get me so far. No matter how many times I rewrote my stories and experiences from a rational perspective, I wouldn't fully understand my beliefs, and how they impacted my decisions, until I faced them. That meant if I really wanted to heal, I could no longer rationalize fear, pain, and the feelings of being unloved. I had to actually feel them instead.

Problem was, I had spent so much of my life trying to repress and manage my emotions that even the thought of allowing them to surface was scary. As an accomplished "sensitive soul" and "drama queen," I'd spent most of my energy disregarding my feelings and pushing down my reactions. I didn't know that fine, okay, and bearable weren't the only emotions that deserved to be expressed. In fact, to do so felt not fine, not okay, and definitely not bearable.

Makes sense—emotions are scary. We fear that they will make us do things we don't think are possible, pressure us into doing things we don't want to do, and stop us from doing the things we dream of. There is no pill we can take to remove them and no switch we can flip to regulate them. Even if we think we can manage them through different practices, they don't go away; they are merely muted. They are always telling us something, regardless of whether we want to acknowledge it. And not only can we not control our own, we definitely can't control other people's.

But what we fail to remember is that emotions are transitory. Whether joy or pain, the emotion itself is fleeting because it exists in a moment in time. Emotions are meant to pass through us like a wave and dissipate once acknowledged. That is because they only exist to let us know how we feel about certain things. Sure, a harder break leaves deeper scars, and a joyous moment leaves an lasting smile, but either way, they are only temporary. They are simply the bridge that takes us to the next moment, when we can experience them again, either in reality or in memory alone. The only emotions that stick around are the difficult ones, and they only do so because when we are running away from them, they have to grow louder and last longer to be heard.

But emotions aren't the source of the pain; they are just the way we receive information. That's why there's no need to fear our emotions. They don't last forever unless we hold on to them forever and ignore the information we are receiving. And the minute their job is done, they dissipate.

I believed that the pain would kill me (literally), so I wasn't about to invite it in. Instead, I committed to the search for someone (or something) else to swoop in and save me from it. In fact, I had gone as far as telling myself that it was my fault the negative emotions existed in the first place because I hadn't controlled them enough. Thing is, as much as I tried, they wouldn't let up—until I was left with no choice but to listen to them.

It wasn't a big moment, a huge hurt, or a crushing disappointment that pushed me to Go Dark. I had just become so tired of blocking the Shit out of my mind that I could no longer keep pretending. I had no more coping mechanisms, fantasies, or excuses to keep them at bay. But when I couldn't even do that anymore, I felt like a failure, and all my other failures rose up to greet me: the failure to meet the expectations I had for myself; the failure of not being strong enough to hold on to love; the failure of admitting that life wasn't worth living if I wasn't deemed lovable by anyone, including myself.

To Go Dark is never easy. It means having to face every ounce of shame, sadness, hurt, and pain. But we do it to grieve for the person we thought we were and to invite in the person we want to be. It's still grief, though: the grief over having allowed ourselves to be small, the grief of the cuts that shaped our perceptions, the grief that it wasn't the way we thought it should be, and the grief that we won't be that person anymore. I knew that I would never be the same again; I just didn't know how the experience would change me.

Yet, the incontrovertible truth is that we can't live fully in the light until we've come fully through the dark. And in allowing myself to Go Dark, I learnt that our emotions, when we dare to feel them, are the true path to freedom. My fear told me that owning my karmic theme would make it my only possible reality, but that wasn't the case at all. It was the opposite. It was about allowing the dark to show me the light.

All I had to do to reach the other side was remember that allowing my emotions was simply an experience, not a permanent state of being. But the more I put off going dark, the less likely I would ever be free of it. So when I could finally just listen to my emotions, I discovered that they weren't telling me I was unhappy because I was an unhappy person. They were telling me I was unhappy because I felt unlovable. But again, feeling something isn't a permanent state of being. Feeling unlovable is not who we are, it merely points to the fact that something is amiss. The moment I realized what was missing, I was able to see that I wasn't unlovable at all—that pain I had been avoiding was actually showing me my desires, my truth, and the next step on my path.

I saw that whilst I didn't have love in ways I expected, I experienced love in unexpected ways. When I felt love for someone else, it was because I was capable of love. When it didn't feel right, I walked away because somewhere inside I believed I deserved better. When it mattered, I loved myself enough to listen. And like a snowball, it grew from there.

As the pain dissipated, something else took its place. I remembered those who had loved me, including those whom I'd forgotten because they didn't fit in the story. But I didn't just remember them; I felt their love too. In fact, I could find love in every relationship, with every person who had significantly impacted me, even the ones who hurt me. Because whether that love was still between us, being able to remember it meant that it still existed.

Then I heard my heart. It was still beating, and it was keeping me alive. I noticed my legs were still carrying me when I walked, my hands were there to break my fall, my immune system was still protecting me, and I was still breathing. Here I was, searching everywhere for unconditional love, believing it never existed, and it was already living inside of me—it was me. My body already loved me enough to keep me alive. My heart didn't just know love, it literally beat for it. It kept me alive, and I was living for it. Love was everything about who I was, and that couldn't change.

By ignoring the dark, every day and in every decision, I kept myself there, never allowing myself to see whether it was true. Had I not confronted it, I would have just continued to have it reflected back at me through my choices. I would still be reacting to it, rather than integrating it and leaving it behind.

I had finally understood what my pain had been trying to show me all along. It wasn't that I was unlovable (like my fear of the dark wanted me to believe), it was just that I wanted more love than my limited understanding of it would allow. To get there, I had to use my emotions in the way they had been designed: to light my path and go through the dark, not around.

Turns out my fate wasn't sealed in the way I had feared. It was only the fear of a future that hadn't yet come, and one that I doubted may never come, that was holding me back. I wasn't broken, I was alive, and I didn't want to stop living because I didn't want to stop loving. I finally knew what I wanted: more love.

Sex & Candy
Liz

As a society, we are obsessed with sex. It drives many of our relationships and underpins many of our interactions. At its essence, sex is creation, but its significance has been diminished by establishing rules and governing it with shame. We've allowed it to become distorted by attaching virtue and judgment to it. What's worse, we continue to distort sex for younger generations because we are unable to face the many issues surrounding it.

Sex is also power. It is the most powerful act we can perform as humans because it connects us to our co-creative power. Co-creative power is the ability to create anything from our own being (it is co-creative in this case because we do not have sex alone; for more information about sex and power, check out our Let's Talk Dirty podcast episodes). That power has less to do with making babies and more about accessing the power we have to bring anything into our immediate reality, which is even greater than creating another life (which is a pretty spectacular gift). It allows us to transform our entire lives and thus our entire world. To tap into or operate from the place of creation, we are opening the door to our divine selves. And it is from that very point that we are able to own our most powerful selves.

However, most of us haven't been able to get there, even if we've been having sex, because we haven't approached it holistically. But how can we if we've never really understood what sex is truly about on a deeper level?

Our inability to understand its power comes from not being able to own our sexuality; but it isn't about sexual orientation or preferences. Rather, it means owning the fact that we are sexual beings who not only crave or desire sexual connection but need it, too. Denying how much we need it has stifled us. In an effort to not be controlled by our sexual nature, we've suppressed it to the point that it's become distorted and unhealthy, and we've repressed ourselves to the extent that sex has become something we've been taught to fear (whether it is the judgment from others, the rules surrounding it that can cause shame, or the idea that we need to suppress our natural desires).

To manage this fear, we've allowed ourselves to become sexual robots. Just as easily as we arrived into this world (thanks to sex!), we've been playing out carefully assigned roles that uphold specific societal norms.

In order to weaken our power, our sexual lives (orientation, act, purpose behind it) have been controlled, commodified, and policed by others. However, by allowing our sexual lives to be governed and dictated, we've allowed our power to be stemmed. And it's often from this disempowered place that many of us approach sex, treating it as something ordinary: a physical, and often shameful, act that results in an inevitable (or so we hope) orgasm.

But as Oneness consciousness surfaces, we are seeing identities and roles become more fluid, and gender matters less than before. Sex is becoming less criminalized, and expressing sexual desires is becoming more mainstream among many cultures.

However, for all the tolerance and openness that's emerging, so are all the hang-ups, misgivings, and shame we've held onto for generations. This is because there is not only individual but also collective karma around sex, which is why we can't stop thinking about it, talking about it, pursuing it, or just plain doing it (or at least trying to get some). Considering how long we've been engaging in sex, we would think we'd be experts at it by now. Instead, most of us hide behind our desks, in the bathroom stalls, or under the covers watching other people pretend to orgasm in contrived juvenile fantasies.

These fantasies keep us stuck, feeding on the idea that the orgasm is enough and that however we are getting it is less important than the orgasm itself—which is far from the truth. Because the truth is, what we want more than anything is to be in that place of connection, of co-creation, to be that divine person in the midst of beautiful chaos and freely experiencing joy on all levels of our being. We just need to get better about it and at it. That begins with unlearning all the Shit we've had instilled in us to repress our natural desires.

Free love, swinging, and all the kinds of relationships that flow along the sexual spectrum are nothing new, original, or even inventive. For many, they merely exist under the radar. Because unless they're socially acceptable, discretion is necessary. But these kinds of relationships are all emerging now, bubbling up to the surface for us to see, experience, and heal. For too long, we've allowed our sex to be judged, internalizing what's "good" and "bad" about sex and thereby limiting the experience. We're expected to *love* our sexual partners, if only for a night. If we don't *love* them, then we're "sluts," "whores," and "players." We've all judged and been judged for our sexual lives. Each. And. Every. One. Of. Us. Sex has been so entwined with our identities; as sexual beings, we have allowed ourselves to be labeled, and that label tells us where we belong in society—until now.

As rules continue to disappear, social structures break down, and the polarities of our world disintegrate, our emerging consciousness of love and tolerance accepts it all. Yet we're not quite ready for what this means. We've been locked in this childish game of hide and seek, hiding from our sexual nature yet seeking connection. We've been fucking absent of real emotion or spirit. We've lost so much faith that we can be loved or love ourselves enough that we have resigned ourselves to fucking a virtual stranger we don't even want from a dating app.

We're not to blame for this. Just as much as we don't have many loving relationships modeled for us, we don't have healthy sexual contact modeled either. And it's not about being able to watch people do it. It's about being able to talk about it, to see titillating images without a sense of guilt or shame—watching healthy, consensual relationships play out on screens or in erotica that stimulate the imagination and remind us of what we already know (this is different from the artificial nature of porn which exploits desire with unrealistic fantasy).

Sex is natural. As humans, it's as natural to us as breathing. Both are essential to our being and becoming. Not only are we at the center of all creation in the act of sex, but we are also transcending our being and becoming something greater because sex is Oneness.

However, for many, sex is the opposite. It's Separation. It's violence. It's validation. It's sacrifice. It's the price we've paid to be women over generations. It's the sacrifice of men for power. For all the reasons sex is healthy, there are many experiences that speak to the contrary. It has damaged many of us beyond what we perceive can be repaired.

We treat sex like a game and play it over and over, repeating the same cycle until it becomes meaningless. But it's as far from meaningless as it can be. It's the very source of our being, which means it matters a great deal. Yet our maturity level speaks to how we treat sex. Do we trade it as currency? Do we surrender it for power? Do we give it up to validate our existence? Yes, yes, and yes. The idea of what sex should be has been shoved down our throats to the point that we've choked on its meaning.

If we're treating sex merely as a pleasurable, biological experience (which it certainly can be), then that's all it will be. It will not transcend us into something greater, which was always its purpose: to bring us to creation, and the source of that creation, which we are at our core. But when we reach our core (as discussed in Chapter Eight), we are forced to confront our unresolved issues. This is why we've often wrapped up our sexual experiences in pain without realizing it. It reminds us of our karma. Because when we're connected, we're present, and to be present means to be fully aware of our unhealed pain. And when there is unhealed pain, any attempt to assuage it through sex will merely bring it to the fore instead.

So many of us avoid the deeper experience of sex and stick with the physical aspect because it's easier, albeit more vacuous. Or we wind up in sexless partnerships and marriages because we'd rather not face the pain or risk of disrupting our ordered lives. Or we avoid it altogether, going cold and celibate rather than connecting with our true selves. Sex brings us to our pain but cannot heal it. Only we can heal ourselves through love. But if we're not coming from a place of love within ourselves, we will act out. And that's no fun.

Sex is fun. Sex, orgasm, and connection are all hallmarks of Oneness consciousness because they bring us into being, into all of our bodies simultaneously: our physical, mental, emotional, and spiritual bodies. When we're with someone who closely matches our vibration in at least one or more of our bodies, sex is great. The more in sync our bodies are with a partner, the greater the experience. And the more in sync we are, the more love we experience because connection is an essential precursor to love.

The message that we need to love the person we're having sex with isn't totally off, but it's not to say we have to be *in* love with the person, we just have to love ourselves enough to be discerning when choosing our sexual partners. Yet it requires maturity to not only take ownership of our bodies but also our healing.

Gimme Some Lovin'
Rhea

When I was young, my mother sat me down and explained the birds and the bees. She used words like "ovaries" and "seeds" and explained scientifically how the whole thing went down. Three days later, I was sitting with my older cousin and she told me where the seeds came from, where the ovaries were located, and how they found each other. It blew my mind.

Shocked that my mother had been misled, I ran downstairs and proceeded to explain in detail, to both my parents, what sex actually was—so they wouldn't get it wrong again (it didn't cross my mind that the fact that I was explaining sex to them meant that they knew exactly what sex was and what it could create). They swallowed their laughter whilst I went into very unnecessary graphic detail about all the parts my mother had missed out. And then I left their room, comforted by the knowledge that they were now up to speed.

It's safe to say, my relationship with sex started with a bit of a misunderstanding. Problem was, I continued to misunderstand it long after that incident took place.

I spent my formative years, as one invariably does, not having sex but being obsessed and scared of it in equal measure. As an adult, that fascination continued, not just personally but professionally as well. (Not only do I have a few degrees that specialize in the subject, but for a while, it's where my career took me.) As a result, I can explain why, as a society, we have a messed-up relationship with sex and consent, why the dysfunction of sex is what sells us products, and why that dysfunction perpetuates our gender stereotypes. Put me in a room with my girls and we can talk about sex all night; but for a long time, if you had put me in a room with someone I was having sex with or wanted to have sex with, I would be mute. (Try describing what you enjoy without using any explicit words; it becomes a weird uncomfortable game of charades.)

Makes sense. In its essence, sex is about connection, desire, and feeling. It is two (or more) people getting as close as they physically can, to the point where their bodies become one. It is the true simultaneous and reciprocal acceptance of one person by another. It is more than gratification; it is spine-tingling, stomach-turning, and toe-curling. It is being so lost in the experience that nothing else matters other than the desire for touch and the satisfaction when that desire is met. And in those moments where our desires have been actualized, our bodies give us the perfect moment of pure peace that is almost nirvana—the orgasm. It is the moment that bridges the abyss between mind, body, and spirit: through the orgasm, we transcend time, silencing everything else other than mutual pleasure.

Sex is literally fucking beautiful.

But just like anything else that requires more than one person and a shred of openness, we have turned sex into an exercise in shame mitigation. Society tells us that there is such a thing as too much, and there is definitely such a thing as too little. If we are too sexy, that's a problem; if no one wants us, that's a problem too. No wonder our views regarding sex are so fucked up. We don't know how to enjoy it.

That's why I rationalized the notion that sex wasn't just a personal problem because I understood that it was a societal problem too. Therefore, until society was in a place where we wouldn't judge sex, there was something I could blame. But it wasn't as simple as that. In fact, I can definitively say that the barometer for how I felt about myself was being reflected back in my relationship with sex, and my interactions with anyone when it came to sex were affected too—so much so, that the more I accepted that I was misunderstanding myself, the more I couldn't deny that I was also misunderstanding sex.

In relationships where I was emotionally insecure, sex was more about the other person's pleasure than my own. It was about being the physical embodiment of their fantasies and the physical experience of their desire. When I was emotionally distant, sex left me feeling empty and, frankly, a little grossed out. When I was emotionally over-involved and had tied it up with a fuck-ton of expectations, it was invariably disappointing. In all three emotional states, without meaning to, sex was used to manage the emotions of myself and others to avoid pain.

I also used sex to curate an impression of myself to connect with others, even those I wasn't sleeping with or those I wanted to sleep with. As a result, I exaggerated my sexploits where appropriate, diminished them where necessary, and freaked out when I had to put any of my talk into action. I had an on-again, off-again relationship with low-cut tops and high heels and an open relationship with sexy underwear, and I convinced myself that my secret fantasies were just that: things to keep secret at all times.

Sex was all about control. It was also the final weapon in my arsenal of hoping to be seen as a catch because I couldn't give it away without careful consideration. As I had done with love, I made sex about who I was and what my worth was (as measured by how fuckable I was, how great it was when it happened, and what everyone thought about me afterward). It became about being chosen, about being attractive, and about being the sexy prize at the end of the playing-hard-to-get tunnel. Mostly, I had made sex an exercise in wrestling with my demons, which made it both exciting (not in an orgasmic way but like I was being put through emotional boot camp) and unappealing because I didn't want to face my issues.

True to form, I found another way to make my interactions with others all about me.

When I convinced myself I was unlovable and undesirable, I told myself that I didn't want to have sex at all because I didn't want to be rejected. I would look at others enjoying sex and pretend to judge, whilst secretly wishing I could own my sexuality. When I started appreciating my body more, sex became approachable and was something to be enjoyed in a controlled environment, that is, an environment with limited emotional fallout. When I owned my desires, I became present and was far more discerning about whom I would consider having sex with. By giving myself permission to fully be in my own body, I started to enjoy everything that it gave me, including the understanding that I was love.

Because that's what sex is, isn't it? We don't just do it to procreate (as my mother implied), it's the physical manifestation of love; not because we are lying on a bed scattered with rose petals and whispering the other person's name whilst they pepper our body with light kisses and wanton thrusts, but because sex allows us to physically express love.

The more we love ourselves, the more comfortable we are and willing to lose ourselves with someone else—and get found in it. When we know who we are and when we choose ourselves first, sex stops being about paying some kind of price for entry and becomes about mutual joy.

But sex also doesn't have to be about being *in* love with the other person either; it's making love, not forcing love. It can be about sharing the love we have with ourselves with someone else, even for one night, without the unnecessary shame hangover the next morning. The more we are able to own who we are and what we want, the more we can remove the societal construct that says we have to be in love with the person to have sex with them.

And that's where the power lies: in that freedom. I had just got it, as usual, a little upside down. The power wasn't in holding sex back as an incentive for someone to chase, keep, hunt, or choose me. It also wasn't about using it as a way to connect without connecting. My power came through owning who I was and embracing my sexuality, in knowing that I wasn't scared to share that love or scared that the other person would leave, taking my love away with them.

Bad Romance
Liz

It may seem antithetical to some that as a spiritual advisor and writer, I also write steamy romance books, but they're a natural extension of my work. Fiction or non-fiction, it doesn't really matter. I write about relationships and love.

It all started after reading *50 Shades of Grey*. I'd never read romance before, put off in part by the wavy-haired, flaxen blondes on the covers of the many (and I mean many) Harlequin paperbacks I shelved while working at a library during high school. But *50 Shades* caught my attention one afternoon during my daughter's swim lesson when a mom with a glazed look in her eyes didn't look up from her copy once in the entire 45 minutes. (It was a good thing there were a few lifeguards in the pool.) I had to know what the big deal was.

After taking the plunge, all the recommendations that mysteriously showed up afterward on my Kindle were romance. And when I poured over the *New York Times* bestseller list, I noticed the number of romance books on the list, in digital and hard copy. I didn't get it until I realized it reflected a lot of what I was seeing in relationships in my spiritual practice. Suddenly, it all fell into place. As the saying goes, life imitates art.

So I read and read some more. I clicked through erotic novellas, trilogies, countless *50 Shades* copycats, and even the lighter stuff. I came away disheartened. If these stories were being consumed regularly (just as they were when I was in high school), then it's no wonder why so many were lost and confused when it came to relationships and love.

So I began to write, and write some more. I experimented by writing a novella that turned into a trilogy that begot another trilogy followed by another. Just when I thought it was time to turn my attention to a different genre because I was tired of trying to find euphemisms for pussy and cock, I wrote a spin-off series.

I played with tropes, all the classic ones: alpha male, billionaire, athlete, professor, student, friend-to-lovers, and cowboy, to name a few. I made the characters less idealized and more human (while still keeping the hot and sexy fantasy bit). Men with flaws were acceptable; assholes who needed a woman's love to turn them around were not. Women were educated and empowered, not weak virgins with daddy issues.

None of my characters used sex as currency, and no one lost their self-respect in the process of discovering love. No one cried while performing a blow job, and no one was raped. There didn't need to be a Happily Ever After (HEA) because people were generally content in spite of their struggles. And not everyone in the story was white. Ultimately, my goal was to counter the negative energy that existing romance books were propagating and bring light to the romance genre. Needless to say, I didn't quit my day job.

In the meantime, I would see clients who would ask me when the One would come. They would also ask what he or she would look like. Tall? Good looking? Well off? (There's always a list.) They'd wonder aloud whether they were destined to be alone while everyone around them was coupled up. They'd ask if the person they were living with was really the One. They'd confess to cheating on their spouses and wanting out. Ultimately, all they wanted to know was if things would ever get easier. They wanted to know if they would have an HEA of their own.

And the answer, inevitably, was yes and no.

Yes, there truly is someone for everyone. No joke. Remember how in Chapter Five I mentioned contracts and how the people who come into our lives bring us lessons? Even our life partners are meant to be part of that. We didn't come into this life to experience and learn about love to have it kept from us. That was never part of the deal. But it could be that we have many *Ones*; the One to teach us to open our hearts; the One who opens us up to discovering ourselves better; the One who invites us to explore those hidden places inside we lacked the courage to face; the One who is sensitive enough to give us space to heal old wounds.

So while we may have a life partner with whom we'll spend many years, possibly 'til death, it's likely that before that person arrives, we'll have plenty of other *Ones* as well. And it may be that we marry someone we thought could be the One, only to outgrow them and end the relationship. No matter the outcome, each and every One of them is intended to bring us to love. And the closer we get to ourselves through those experiences, the closer we come to being with someone whom we can partner our lives and purpose with.

Partnership in our lifetime is about purpose. The clearer we are about who we are and why we are here—even if we don't know our actual purpose or understand where we're going—brings us closer to our partners. The more honest we can be about it, the closer we get. The more of our pain, hurt, and wounding we can heal, the fewer barriers we will encounter. If our ultimate purpose is to come into our divinity, which we do through love and joy, then our partnership must represent both of those in the deepest ways possible.

This is where the pursuit of romance's HEA complicates things. If we're focused on the HEA, we're not living our purpose. We're putting our eggs into one basket, writing our endings before we've figured out the plot. But our motivation as characters in the story of our lives is to come into love and subsequently our divinity, and the plot is our personal journey to which there is no end. That means that all the characters who enter our stories, chapter by chapter, further us along that path. As a result, the HEA doesn't come when we find our life partner, just as our lives don't suddenly start the moment we ride off into the proverbial sunset.

Our HEAs come when we realize we never needed them in the first place.

This is because there is really no such thing as a HEA in the form of another person. The One was always us. But fairy tales, romances, and rom-coms made us believe otherwise. The love they teach isn't really love at all but a distorted shadow of what love is meant to be.

Romance loves fixer-upper scenarios. The person isn't enough until we make them enough for us, either through sacrifice, hard work, or money. And once they're enough for us, then it means we're enough. We've found our redemption through another person. But no matter how we do it, we're forgetting the big lesson karma teaches us: no one will be enough for us until we are enough for ourselves. Until then, all that is being reflected back is those shattered mirror images of one another and the ego-driven plot lines that do not speak of the higher love of which we are all capable.

Furthermore, romance and rom-coms use some form of the fairy tale formula: unrealistically gorgeous people; grandiose gestures; broken people needing saving; and heroes (emotional and physical) needing someone to save. But this isn't what love is. Love is Oneness. It is recognizing ourselves in another. This is only possible between two whole and healed people. It does not mean that a person can't have wounds that need tending to but that they are healed enough to be able to stand on their own emotionally. If they are not, what we wind up with is only a diminished version of the person they are meant to be.

To be enough for ourselves is to recognize that we are our HEA. We are the One in Oneness, which means we are Love. Love cannot be expressed or displayed simply by a series of prescribed acts, gestures, or words. To assume it can immediately reduces it. We come into love by recognizing that beyond our perceived brokenness, flaws, and imperfections, true perfection is at our core. And our partner, whoever they are, mirrors that perfection, which makes them perfectly suited to us.

But if we cannot recognize we are enough, whoever we encounter on our journey won't be enough, either. This takes growing up. It takes throwing out the old paradigms of relationships that formed the foundation of what we took for love. It means allowing Romance to die the death it needed four generations ago, to allow a new concept of Love to take root in our hearts and grow.

Enabling this kind of mature love requires us to take responsibility for ourselves. To be responsible for ourselves means we cannot hide behind fantasies and the false hope that things will be better when we meet the One. It means understanding that no one else will save us because no one else can save us. And it's scary because, like children, we don't want to leave the nest or the security of the familiar and the predictable. We'd all prefer to stay in the comfort of our beds just a little longer.

Unfortunately, we can't continue to hit *snooze* anymore; not if we want something different from what we already have; not if we want stronger, more enriching relationships than many of us have known or experienced. But to do this, we have to believe in ourselves, believe we are capable, and believe we are strong enough to write a new story—an original one that hasn't been rehashed a thousand times, made possible when we realize that we are our own hero.

You're All I Need To Get By
Rhea

I have always been a love-story enthusiast. Fiction or nonfiction, I enjoy hearing how people met, what obstacles they overcame, and how they fell in love. I can devour at least two *chick-lit* novels a week, and I've seen nearly every romantic comedy out there. As a result, I can say with complete authority that when it comes to romance, I get it. At the start of every story, both are broken in some way (that makes them relatable because… who isn't?) and from the falling in love, to out of love, and back in love, to the will-they-won't-they (they inevitably do), and everything in between that tends to happen on a sandy beach, they always find their HEA, usually having mind-blowing sex along the way.

What I didn't fully appreciate is that even those stories weren't about me, indulging in them while going through my own "ups and downs" was an issue. I already believed that I had to change myself to find a relationship, and consuming these love stories offered the validation that I was right to do so. I was also assured that I would be *good enough* once I had found the One. Those stories morphed from fantasy and escape into a solution. And it was a solution that was definitely worth the wait, the reasoning, and the effort.

Without meaning to, other people's ideas of what love should be (to explain why they didn't need to deal with their own Shit) replaced my blueprint. They became part of my hoped future and had me wondering why I hadn't found my own HEA yet. I took it personally, convincing myself that it was my fault that the One hadn't appeared or stuck around. I made it about earning them, either by being perfect or by being broken. I wasn't sure which one, but it was definitely one or the other (so I was trying to be both).

That's how romance or any HEA story fucks us up. As fun as they are to read, we end up creating a whole bunch of "shoulds" and then apply those rules to our own relationships—whether it's how someone is supposed to behave, what makes an ideal candidate for romance, how we illustrate our affection, or what happens at the end of the story. We absorb someone else's opinions on what relationships should be, and in doing so, we ensure they no longer belong to us at all.

I made it impossible to recognize the person for who they were because I was drowning them with the stories in my head. I believed love was in the ups and downs, the dramatic, the immediate, the addictive, and the inescapable. I thought my hero would look and act like heroes: say all the right things, treat me like a queen, and take all of my crap with a smile. Better yet, they would fix themselves because I was a *good enough* motivation to do so and it would fix me as a result.

That meant that all the things that I actually wanted in a partner fell by the wayside. The consistent ones were boring, the kind ones were needy, and the ones who were responsible for themselves were unicorns. Because in every failed love story I experienced, I wrote another requirement to explain why he hadn't come before. Soon, my list of requirements was so specific that it was unlikely they could actually exist.

In fact, even if the One had actually shown up at my door, it wouldn't have changed anything. I would have been too resentful, frustrated, and passive-aggressive because he took his damn time. Or I would have been waiting for him to figure out that I wasn't deserving of him, whilst looking out for all the ways he wasn't deserving of me either; all so that I could justify why I was better off when he decided he'd had enough and I was single again.

But I wasn't meant to be this unhappy waiting for someone else. And no one, not even a figment of my imagination, was worth the price of my unhappiness—especially since I had already given myself permission to Go Dark and see that I had experienced more love than I was willing to admit and that I wanted more love than my current situation allowed. In fact, I was the hero for facing my own demons and confronting my pain. I wasn't broken, but by buying into these love stories, I was breaking myself into parts, all so that I could make myself fit.

Whether it was fiction or nonfiction, the further I got sucked into other people's explanations of what love was, the further I got from my own experience of it. Except my life wasn't someone else's to write, so my love story wasn't going to come from them either. My life was messy, hard, fun, and great. I was never going to be perfect, and neither was the other person. In buying into the Shit of what our love should look like, I was ruining the potential of what it could be for both of us.

Our potential could never be realized if I was limiting my own. Because even though these typical love stories ended with a bang, I had a feeling that a real love story had no end. So by releasing myself from the story, not only could I start a new one, but I could also write it as I went along. I was ready to learn how to write my own story, trust that no matter what it looked like I would be able to keep going, and finally believe that I would know love when I found it.

Prove Your Love
Rhea

After I saw my fears for what they were, I understood that my mind had been an accomplice to my unhappiness. I had believed my mind was working for me, but in looking out for every pitfall and avoiding them, I created even more.

Not only was this draining, but it split me in two. Whenever I had an impulse to do something from my heart, or a feeling that things could work out, my mind immediately overruled it due to a lack of evidence and an overactive negative confirmation bias. So, when my heart told me something and my mind shut it down to avoid pain, a disconnect was subconsciously being recognized, no matter how much I tried to out-think it, excuse it, or explain it away.

If I had any hope for sanity (and different results), I could no longer allow my mind to overrule my heart. Even though my mind helped mitigate my fears, as long as my fears were in charge, I always felt like Shit. Allowing myself to Go Dark wasn't the high point of my "healing journey," but as a result of the very dramatic cry-fest, I cleared out the old emotions and got the clarity I needed. It wasn't my desire for love that hurt me, it was that I wasn't getting the kind of love I wanted. But to get that love, I had to learn to navigate my life from a new place, which wasn't free from emotions; rather, it was informed by them.

That meant I needed to see what would happen if I actually listened to my heart instead. The challenge was that I had to understand that emotions weren't necessarily a "bad" thing that would lead me down the rabbit hole of "wrong" decisions. Rather, they were there to keep me aligned to what I was seeking (took me six years, eight drafts of this chapter, and countless sighs from Liz to figure that one out). I hoped that it wouldn't all blow up in my face, but I already knew that anything was better than living in a place of fear and consistently reaffirming that fear.

Behaving a certain way "because I had a feeling" was new for me. For someone like me who always relied on her mind, it felt like launching myself out of an airplane without a parachute. So, whilst I listened to my intuition telling me to leap, I still assessed that feeling, rather than actually feeling it. That meant I would invariably overthink myself into a spiral and second-guess everything, trying to figure out which decision came from the heart and which was dictated by my mind. And when it came time to actually leap, I closed my eyes, prayed I didn't land on my face, and said "Fuck This" on what seemed like my way down.

Dating from this mixed-up place became even more confusing than it had been before, and I wasn't getting the results I hoped for. I didn't trust my choices (because I didn't know what to do) and, as a result, I connected with people who didn't trust themselves either and were therefore just as untrustworthy as I believed myself to be. I invented tests to see if they deserved my trust without realizing that no matter what someone else did or said, even if they were telling the truth, I wouldn't believe them. Not that it mattered. They would flake constantly, lie casually, or make excuses because life was "too stressful." In the end, I jumped to conclusions that weren't there, and I never sat still for long enough to ask myself if I actually wanted to stick around.

I didn't see that every time I broke a boundary and every time they broke a promise, we were telling each other that we couldn't be trusted. And whenever they spoke in riddles and I connected dots that didn't exist, whatever faith I had slowly faded. But I didn't dare ask myself if my approach was working for me. I didn't think I had another choice. Any rejection would have validated my fears that I couldn't change my circumstances. So, I spent my time avoiding any type of "no," and in doing so, it took away every shred of confidence when I got a "yes"—further compounding the problem and rendering me impotent.

When we can't trust ourselves to make a choice, or default to the one that feels safe, that lack of trust is reflected back to us in everything we do and say, and even by the people we connect to. Like attracts like (more on this later), so when we don't have the clarity to listen to ourselves, we easily attract others who do the same. Our Shit meets their Shit to create the perfect Shitshow.

I didn't have a heart or mind problem, I had a Shit problem. Choosing one part of me over the other (whether it was my heart or my mind) was actually choosing the fear that I wasn't *good enough*. Yet, by not dealing with it, I left myself straddling some kind of twisted middle ground where nothing could substantially change.

Without allowing my heart and mind to operate together the way in which they needed to, I would never be able to realize the results I really wanted. I asked my mind to feel and my heart to prove itself through logic and reason. I treated them as if they were two distinct things, challenging each one to prove their worth, whilst determining their value based on which one provided better results. But my mind couldn't feel and my heart didn't think. So, even though my mind and heart had the same goal (which was for me to get to the kind of love I was seeking), in prioritizing one over the other, I prevented them from working harmoniously in order to achieve that. It's no wonder I ended up back where I didn't want to be.

Let Your Love Flow

To put it plainly, I didn't trust that anything would ever change. And because I'd been so used to not getting what I wanted or what I felt was meant to come to me, I doubted it ever would. But, as much as I wanted a different outcome, despite my best intentions, I still approached things from a place of control. Only this time I listened to my heart to spite my mind. Yet, in dismissing my mind entirely, and by choosing one part of myself over the other, I was pitting myself against myself and hoping that I'd come out unscathed.

As Liz and I have mentioned in our podcast, there are four pillars of Trust. *Trust* is that everything happens for our highest good (everything we have done, everything we do, and everything we will do will bring about the most beautiful and joyful life that is possible, knowing that we create it for ourselves). *Faith* is the firm conviction that there is something out there that has our back. *Knowing* is the instant recognition or unwavering understanding of our core truth. And *Hope* is the reflection of our heart's desires. These pillars make up the foundation of Love.

Thing is, we can't come into Trust when we've split ourselves into pieces. We spend our time at war with ourselves, ensuring that the one thing we want is the one thing we can't get to. That's the thing about fear. The uncertainty and lack of faith in ourselves are mirrored back until we wake up and realize that we're contributing to the dissonance of what our lives look like and what we want them to be.

By not trusting that I could Trust, I distorted it into some bullshit learn-through-pain thing, turning my life into an endurance test whilst assuring myself that it would make sense later to make it bearable. Until I understood I was both my heart and my mind, I couldn't trust myself, and my fears wouldn't go anywhere. In fact, I gave them free rein to keep telling me I was the problem, thus cementing the idea that nothing would change regardless of what I did.

My world would never shift if I couldn't *trust* myself to act in accordance with my highest good, have *faith* in myself despite feeling let down by things outside of my control, access my *knowing* that all my efforts were moving me towards my happiness, and *hope* that it would all play out to my benefit, rather than to my detriment. Without these four pillars, my entire world was as flimsy as a house of cards.

Only when I finally saw that my fear of not being *good enough* to be loved was the problem could I work towards the solution. And that solution came from both my heart and my mind because that same goal they shared was to be in love. My heart wanted to connect to more love and my mind translated that to mean another person. They had both been searching for the same thing in their own ways. Even though my mind had been misguided as to how I would find that love, getting to love was still the one thing they agreed on. Finally, the aha moment (that had been staring me in the face the whole time) gave me the starting point to trust that I would get somewhere.

Trust isn't something we just decide to do one day out of the blue, just as much as we don't fall blindly into love. Trust, like love, comes from us first; and, like love, it also grows. We start by choosing it every day and in every action until it becomes who we are. Initially, it's the small things, such as holding ourselves accountable, saying what we mean, and doing what we say. It's not betraying ourselves the moment we have to be honest with ourselves or another person just because we don't know what will happen next. It's listening to ourselves and honoring every single part of us, even if they don't make sense. It may start as a concerted effort, but it eventually develops into a habit until it becomes immutable (or, as I like to say, "experience makes normal"). It may be difficult for us to do something new for the first time, especially when it involves challenging a fear that we hold, but the more we do something, the more natural it becomes.

Trust is also the mechanism by which we create connections, first with ourselves and then with others. Once I understood that my heart and mind had the same goal, they trusted one another a little more. But I still needed to see that trust in action for it to be cemented. Whether it was sending that crazy text at 2 a.m., expressing myself honestly, or saying yes to something that felt right even though it was fucking scary, I saw that things could work out differently. This gave me the courage to keep going. And the more space my mind gave to my heart to be heard, the more it understood that there was more than one possible outcome in every scenario.

In trusting that my heart and mind could work together, and following through, I vanquished the fears that kept me tied to a reality I didn't want. In listening to myself, I was no longer at war within and finally felt at peace. I wouldn't have been able to truly believe that it was possible until I saw it in action, but in exercising Trust, I connected my heart and mind to facilitate their ultimate goal, which was to get me to my highest good. My karma wasn't for my highest good. Challenging it, confronting it, and figuring out how to make it my bitch was. And Trust was the key to doing it.

Trust wasn't anything to fear. Following my heart wasn't nearly as dangerous as I had once believed. My choices couldn't be dictated by how the other person responded to me or what would happen next. As long as I felt aligned with myself, it didn't matter where or how I landed. I would always end up in a better place than where I started. In fact, a lot of my second-guessing was just another way to attach a story to a feeling that couldn't be deciphered but would eventually become clear.

That's the thing about Trust. We can't predict where it leads us because we can't control, manipulate, target, or shape the outcome. But it leads us to all the places we wish we could go but never really believe are possible. We can't always plan or see the steps we need to take to get there, but we can use our power to create the life we desire and facilitate it for ourselves. And when we get to a place where Trust is a given, not only do we get to play but, no matter what happens, we also never lose.

It's a Damn Shame
Liz

Fear of missing out (FOMO) is a global epidemic because we have all carried the same deeply rooted fear of not being *good enough*. Earlier generations didn't experience FOMO so acutely because they were living according to rules, paradigms, gender roles, and social mores around which they structured their lives. They weren't feeding on the flood of images and stories presented 24/7, nor were they bombarded with ads to the overwhelming degree we are today.

Thanks to the internet, our world and our perception of it have shifted entirely. Everything appears to be at our fingertips. Life-changing adventures seem within reach, and the world seems smaller than before, which makes us more aware of our connection to one another. In our social media feeds, we can know what's going on anywhere at any time, and where people are at any given moment. Yet, while we seem so much more connected than ever before, we're also becoming aware how divided we still are.

What drives this Separation and feeds the core fear of *I Am not Good Enough* is FOMO because our outside world is always a reflection of our internal one. If we fear that we are not *good enough*, we will always look at what others have and find ourselves lacking, or we will attempt to emulate their success instead of defining our own. But so long as we've experienced Separation within, we've had Separation with-out. As a result, we've lived in a hierarchical state of constant division, from economic status and education to race and physiology where much of the consolidated power resides at the top.

As our consciousness evolves, we recognize this doesn't have to be the case. As we come into greater wholeness and healing, we see how much damage these hierarchies have wrought. And as we become aware of our own personal power (and how long we've sublimated it), the less inclined we are to surrender it to others. But most of us are not completely there yet. We're still stuck in the karmic loop of not being *good enough*, which means we haven't tackled what keeps us locked in it: shame.

Shame is what keeps us separate from ourselves and our purpose. It is the internalized story of not being *good enough*. It tells us that whatever economic, social, or racial barriers we face are impossible to overcome. It reminds us of our fear that no matter how hard we try, we don't have what it takes. It also reinforces the self-doubt, the insecurities, and the fears that underscore our daily lives because we aren't sure how our appearance, manner of speech, or body language will be perceived.

We've all been judged and labeled at some point, but all these labels limited us to the spectrum of narrowly defined character traits, to keep us in line and fit into roles. Being judged makes us all too focused and aware of what we aren't, as opposed to what we are (and could be), further keeping us in our karmic loop.

When we are not X, then we need to be Y. If we're not *good enough*, then we need to find a way to make ourselves acceptable, and so we look to someone else to define it for us. We're sold an idea, a product, or a lifestyle that we're convinced will somehow improve us by making us prettier, sexier, appealing, smarter, richer, or stronger. Except, we are not meant to be everything. We are not meant to be like everyone else. We are meant to be ourselves. We are meant to recognize that our perfections don't come from being perfect but rather from perfecting who we are. That means being ourselves to the fullest.

To do this takes knowing ourselves, and to know ourselves means sifting through our layers of pain and suffering to get there. It requires that we confront the messages we internalized about not being *good enough* and replace our fears with love. Only then can we fully own who we are and connect to our purpose.

FOMO keeps us from our purpose. It locks us in the *if only* mindset: if only I did… if only I'd have… if only I had… if only I were… This happens so readily because many of us still operate within a hierarchical paradigm. We've lived in it for too long, and it's so embedded within our subconsciousness that it's difficult, nearly impossible, not to. But as long as we continue to look outside of ourselves by choosing to model or mimic those who seem to have what we do not, we will never be able to get to our purpose.

If we want to make karma *our* bitch, to improve our lives, have fulfilling relationships and careers, as well as do what it is we came to do during our short time on this planet, then it's time to see FOMO for what it is: a symptom of our shame. This begins with deciding that we are enough as we are, no matter our flaws or imperfections.

Road to Nowhere

Most of the approaches to self-improvement have been more damaging to us than many of us realize. This is because they keep us striving towards external validation, pushing us through the FOMO pipeline, while continuing to prop up those with the power to influence how we live, think, and perceive others (especially in relation to us). And so long as we're emulating other people's purpose (everyone's an entrepreneur, life coach, astrologer, or armchair therapist these days), we are not only surrendering our power, but we are also perpetuating a hierarchy that keeps us small.

Learning to listen to ourselves is a simple concept that isn't necessarily easy to do. We *could* unplug ourselves from social media, but that would only be a temporary fix. We *could* rationalize our purpose (to serve, to teach, to help, to heal), but unless we can fully embody it by connecting true emotion to it, then it's like any other job and won't be fulfilling. We *could* think about what makes us happy and turn that into our purpose. But since our limited experience of happiness tends to be more transient in nature, that purpose won't bring contentment for long.

What we need to connect to our purpose and reduce FOMO is discernment. Discernment is knowing our highest good. Discernment tells us that while something may look appealing, it may not be for us or bring us the kind of joy it brings someone else. Discernment reminds us that in spite of monumental challenges, only we have the power to work through them. Discernment teaches that no one can do for us what we can do for ourselves. And we can only know what is in our highest good when we know ourselves completely.

One of our greatest challenges today, and for the subsequent generations, is to deal with this FOMO. It will take time and a concerted effort to undo all the many ways in which it affects how we live, think, and relate to one another. Some may choose to undergo a complete life revolution by throwing out everything and starting afresh. Yet, not everyone is in a position to do so. Some need to carefully untangle the way FOMO is woven into their lives to avoid disrupting tenuous relationships and circumstances. To do this requires first removing shame.

Often when we try to remove shame, we feel guilty because it means that all the relationships we have (which underpin our story) must shift, and we don't want to be responsible for that. But if we want to grow, if we want to experience the possibilities life has to offer, then it means embracing the unknown and aligning with our purpose.

Aligning with our purpose makes us outliers because it means eschewing all the conventions established by previous generations. Perhaps we'll get married later or not at all. Maybe we won't have children. Perhaps we'll decide to live in a yurt and work odd jobs instead of a 9 to 5 gig. Maybe we won't get a university degree. Whatever we choose to do with our lives and however we go about it is completely and entirely up to us.

Responsibility is frightening. We've never truly experienced it before. That's what hierarchy did for us and why we supported it. So long as we followed rules and sublimated our power to others to ensure our well-being, we would be safe. All we had to do was fit ourselves into certain boxes to yield a predictable outcome. Yet, our rising consciousness tells us this way of being isn't tolerable anymore. We cannot expect equality or peace if we don't own our power and take responsibility for ourselves.

Responsibility isn't about returning a library book on time, paying the bills, or doing all the things that make us "grown-up." Rather, it's about accepting the fullness of our lives: that we are bigger than and more divine than we ever thought possible (making karma our bitch is the way to get here). This takes truly understanding that we are *good enough* and accepting that we are free to choose every single aspect of our lives, despite the limitations we perceive and the opinions of others. This is true freedom, something few of us have ever really known because we've been too attached to the stories that tell us that we are *good enough* because… or that we'd be *good enough* if only…

And what are we without our stories? We don't yet know. We're only beginning to see the possibilities because it's all happening in real-time. But what we do know is that if we continue to run away from ourselves and our purpose by indulging in FOMO, we won't find out.

Body Talk
Liz

Our bodies speak to us every day. We've just become very adept at ignoring them, which is why, despite all of the medical breakthroughs and advances, our bodies are barely holding it together. In hiding from our worries, fears, and problems, we've buried our bodies in illness, disease, and chronic pain.

From aches, pains, tension, and disease, our bodies are telling us something. We suffer physically because we suffer emotionally. And we suffer emotionally because we suffer spiritually. When we don't acknowledge how connected our physical body is to the other parts of us, we cannot see (yet we deeply experience) our emotional and spiritual selves that we regularly neglect.

But as our symptoms play out through our physical bodies, we become distracted from our actual problems. As a result, we wind up being too busy trying to heal the physical, forgetting to pay attention to the origin of our issue. It's all too easy to ignore our unhappiness, regret, stress, anger, and misery. We've developed a pill for every problem and a procedure for every perceived flaw, and we use numbing agents when reality is too hard to handle, and we rationalize it all. Our bodies have borne the brunt of our self-abuse, and instead of treating them with care, we continually take them for granted.

The connection between our emotional and physical bodies is referred to in our everyday idioms. We cry our hearts out, have to get something off our chest, carry the world on our shoulders, and refer to others as a pain in the neck. We can't stomach something or someone, feel it in our bones, or have a gut feeling. But our lack of vocabulary around our emotional experiences and unwillingness to confront the source of our pain means we stay stuck in the physical loop of our issue—never fully healing one or the other, maintaining and coping until the next problem arises.

The reason we find physical pain and suffering preferable to emotional discomfort is because we believe we can treat it. Our emotional and spiritual selves, on the other hand, are uncharted territory. We don't know what it would take to deal with them, so we'd rather not. In fact, we go months, even years, not dealing with our Shit, so when our bodies try to wake us up, approaching them holistically becomes a daunting task.

We've buried ourselves under so much responsibility that we have too much going on or too many people depending on us, or we have gone too long denying our issues that unpacking them is too daunting. Many of us can't or won't stop our lives in order to heal because we struggle to understand ourselves as emotional and spiritual beings. And it's that disconnect that keeps us at war with our bodies.

We carry on like this until one day we wake up and something doesn't work as well as it used to. Or a tumor is there that wasn't there before. Or an infection comes out of nowhere. Or we're diagnosed with a mystery condition such as an autoimmune disorder. Then our calendars become filled with doctors' appointments, MRIs, and CT scans. Conversations begin to revolve around our medical issues rather than our emotional ones. And the emotional and spiritual problems that originate from our physical ones are shoved even further back and forgotten.

Healing our physical bodies holistically requires us to approach the origin of our spiritual pain. While the root of our karma is not being *good enough*, the origin of our physical pain has everything to do with the story we created to support that belief.

Waking Up

The stress of my karmic story led to my autoimmune disease diagnosis, Hashimoto's, when I was 34 years old. Hypothyroidism and several other autoimmune disorders are the result of the issue: "When is it my turn?"

I was living my life the way I thought best, but while I believed I was taking care of myself and living up to my responsibilities, there was a deeper issue at play that I wasn't able to see. I was too caught up in moving around the world every couple of years, keeping up with my always-busy husband, and taking care of our children. Regular medical check-ups showed I was in good health, so it wasn't clear to me that anything needed to change. My life, for all intents and purposes, was enough.

That was, until I was hit by an inexplicable acne outbreak (the spiritual reason for acne is hiding who we are, since many facial issues relate to how we present ourselves to the world). Since nothing my dermatologist did was effective, he suggested I do some blood work. Sure enough, there was an underlying cause of my acne that had nothing to do with oily skin or clogged pores. The diagnosis devastated me.

While there was the initial relief that whatever was causing my acne could be understood and therefore treated, I grieved for my body. The idea that my thyroid was slowly dying and how that would impact my body was a kick in the stomach. I'd considered myself fairly fit and healthy. I took care of my body by eating healthy, exercising, and having regular check-ups. I was stunned that this could happen.

And then I wasn't. My diagnosis and subsequent grieving woke me up. While I was doing the best I could in my life, I wasn't at my best. Hypothyroidism results from a low-functioning thyroid, which is necessary for helping the body maintain balance. My life was completely and utterly out of balance, especially after the birth of my second child. I was overwhelmed and miserable—as if coming down with shingles when my second child was twelve weeks wasn't enough of a sign. That hurt to admit because, as honest as I was with myself, I'd traded my honesty for positive thinking, expecting that it could influence my emotional state and make that period of my life bearable. I'd become a Pollyanna.

In my later adult years, when I struggled the most, I often sought the silver lining. But I'd been looking at the silver lining for so long, it had blinded me to my reality, which wasn't very happy. I ignored all the unpleasant things about my life and reminded myself that it could always be worse. And I didn't think I had any other choice but to keep going and moving.

I had two very young children who were entirely dependent upon me. We depended on my husband's income to provide for us because I couldn't really work. He depended on his career for his stability because of his unstable childhood and worked extremely long hours and most weekends, meaning he was often absent.

The further his career advanced, the worse the hours. The worse the hours, the more responsible I became for the other areas of our lives—until all the responsibility became less harmonious and the pendulum swung wildly from one end of his misery spectrum to mine. By then, he was so far down his career path, change seemed too scary and unpredictable.

We found ourselves stuck in this traditional marriage paradigm: my husband was the breadwinner while I was the stay-at-home wife, trailing spouse, and mother. And we ended up so far from where we began, there seemed to be no other option but to stay the course.

With every up (new city, new baby!), there was a down (new city, new baby!), and my ability to put myself first diminished. I felt so weighed down by my life that I couldn't acknowledge my suffering. And, since relationships are a mirror, I couldn't see that it was a reflection of my husband's suffering as well.

Figuring that misery is only temporary (after all, every relocation came with an expiration date), we stayed in our individual karmic loops of trying to be *good enough* for ourselves, one another, and our families. But it locked us in this collective story that ironically (although not surprisingly) matched my parents'. My father was in the Navy, so he was rarely around, and my mom worked full time and raised three children (not all details match 100%, but you catch my drift). My parents' unresolved karma had become my story. Karma can truly be a bitch.

The only solution was to break the cycle. For some, that would mean ending a marriage. But I knew better than to equate my husband with his pain. I knew him too well. He'd always had a lot of life force, but he was anchored to a thankless, demanding job and drowning in fear. He wasn't in a good place, and ending things wouldn't have made it any better.

I wasn't in a good place either. In retrospect, I was postpartum and drowning in fear. And we'd become so beholden to the income his career provided that it seemed impossible to question it. Taking a wrecking ball to our lives wasn't just an unappealing option, it wasn't an option at all. The tapestry of our lives was so tightly woven that pulling a single thread would have unraveled it all.

But sometimes a single change is a catalyst for the larger shifts to occur. It just takes time and patience. For every layer of our karmic story we uncover, it takes time to heal and process it, time we don't often think we have because of the arbitrary timelines we impose on ourselves. And when we're miserable, we want it to go away as quickly as possible, so we take the medication or undergo the treatment and hope for the best. Other times we may just throw out everything and start anew, but often that only begets greater destruction. We don't all have the luxury or the constitution for that.

For us, since we were living in Brazil and given our desire not to disrupt our lives any more than they had been, we needed an out that wouldn't result in my husband's immediate unemployment and to land in a city where he could find another job. The eventual move was sudden, but like ripping off a band-aid, it was necessary to promote faster healing. It took us to New York, where our story had begun eleven years before and gave us an enhanced do-over, to experience a more grounded life than our ex-pat one. And like with every move, we were forced to confront old wounds we would have otherwise ignored in the busyness of daily life.

If I hadn't listened to my body, if I'd kept pushing myself by taking on more responsibilities than necessary and searching for the silver lining, I would've faced another health crisis. But once I could see that my physical issues were a symptom of the larger issues that I was afraid to confront, I could do something about it. Because the greater the denial, the harder we need to get hit in order to wake up. This means that we ultimately face a choice: wake up to ourselves and our issues now or gamble with our well-being. It begins by deciding what our priorities are and what we want our futures to look like. Only we can determine what that means to us.

Shiny Happy People
Rhea

I have always felt quite different, and although I wished it never bothered me, for a long time, it really did. I wanted to be like everyone else and live like everyone else, but no matter what I did to treat the dissonance, nothing worked.

Even my perspective on life seemed different from everyone else. I didn't think life had to be about suffering, I thought love made the world go round and I thought magic was a given. But on the rare occasion where I would confide in someone else about how I thought things could be (in contrast to how they were unfolding), they would laugh and ask me whether it hurt when I fell off my unicorn. They would tell me I had become lost in my imagination and that my wildest dreams were just that: dreams. Apparently, life was a lot harder than I was giving it credit for, and the sooner I accepted their reality as opposed to my naive fantasies, the better my life would be.

No wonder I thought I had a "me" problem and that was what needed fixing. How I believed the world could be and how I fit into it was apparently misguided, delusional, or just plain wrong. By all accounts, I was to blame for my suffering because I was the one who was setting myself up for disappointment, simply by believing my own hype.

Instead of listening to my heart, I listened to other people. I observed their lives, habits, and perspectives so that I could adopt them, telling myself that if I could have the same things, the same relationships, and the same friends, then I could be happy like they were. I was the ideal consumer, buying the dress, the smile, and the figure to find my salvation. And I studied other people's stories, not because I was that interested in their lives, but because I wanted the instructions for their success.

I didn't realize it at the time, but my struggles gave me everything I was looking for. In being miserable, I was exactly like everyone else. I just didn't know they were miserable too, partly because they were all so good at pretending that they were fine. We were all trying to play the game better than everyone else, believing that this was how we were going to win.

The problem is, in pretending to be someone else, owing to a lack of confidence to be ourselves, we maintain the fear that we are not *good enough*—whilst thinking we would be *good enough* if only we had a better lifestyle, the ideal partner, or a healthier bank account. In doing so, we lose that connection with ourselves, believing we are only whole when revered by everyone else for being perfect and having all the perfect accessories that come with it (including someone extra special by our side who reflects how great we are because they are perfect too). But in buying into the bullshit, we perpetuate it so that it is the only reality that we know.

Our individual story of being not *good enough* creates a collective one, and the more we adhere to it, the more it becomes a religion. Like devout followers of this Shit of our own making, we stand in judgment of ourselves and each other, silencing our outliers in the pursuit of common morality. And we assign those who belong in heaven as part of that collective (being accepted and being loved) or in hell as an individual (ostracized and alone).

We have effectively corrupted our inherent desire for connection and used it to our detriment, separating ourselves from who we are, simply to become who we think everyone else wants us to be. But as we can't sustain it naturally, we don't just believe that we are not *good enough,* we start to believe that we will never be enough. So we tell ourselves that we are all suffering because that is what it means to be alive.

I lapped up those rules because, in the absence of faith in myself, I needed guidance. I measured myself against others because I needed validation that I was doing a good job. I strived to be the perfect daughter, the perfect sister, the perfect friend, the perfect partner, and the perfect member of society. I was too scared to say no to anything because I thought that withdrawing my utility would result in them withdrawing their affection. I would cancel my own plans in order to do a favor for someone else, swallow my words to not rock the boat, or respond to situations with how I thought others wanted me to. But in putting their needs before my own, I was effectively upholding and elevating someone else's values and negating mine, allowing others to define everything about my existence.

Except I could never trust myself to do anything perfectly whilst outrunning and denying my perceived inherent imperfections. All I could achieve was consistently failing to meet my own twisted expectations. I could never be pretty enough, clever enough, or pliable enough when I was looking at other people to define what enough even meant (especially since everyone had differing opinions). Yet, in failing to question, even for a moment, whether the beliefs I was operating from were the problem, I remained stuck.

Losing My Religion

By allowing social structures to tell me what was right and wrong, I was giving away my heart. By allowing myself to believe I wasn't perfect already, I kept myself searching for absolution—for faults that I couldn't be sure were faults at all. Yes, I was searching for love (or some version of love), which to me was acceptance and connection, but it would never be enough because it didn't start from within me, it started against me. It started from a place where I was ashamed of who I was, rather than from a place where I was connected to myself and my desires. And even if I found what I thought I wanted, I would always be waiting for my next fuck-up that would ensure I would lose it again.

But I always had a choice, and it had always started

and finished with me. I was the one who listened to someone else over myself. I was the one who measured my worth using other people's barometers. I was the one who conformed to everyone else's ideas of what lovable looked like and got lost in the mess. I was the one who kept trying to reach an unattainable standard of perfection so that I wouldn't have to risk being rejected for being me. I was the one to keep doing so, over and over again, even when it clearly wasn't working. My suffering was the result of my choices. I may not have believed I had a choice, but I did. I didn't have to keep trying to fit in, I could choose to be myself.

I may not have known how my world would look if I chose differently, but without trying, I could never know. In refusing to make any different choices, I kept myself in an endless loop of striving for perfection and falling short.

Other people weren't the God that was punishing me, I was. I was the God in my world because my choices and perceptions dictated my experiences. Without seeing heaven could only come from within me, I would forever wait in hell. But I couldn't continue punishing myself for a failed redemption that no one else could provide. In doing so, I would always remain lacking. So in order to find my own heaven, I had to lose the religion I had capitulated to—the collective story of not being *good enough* that was defined by fear and had reinforced my own.

In *A Karmic Introduction,* Liz described the karmic theme *I Am Unlovable* as "I cannot be loved by another because God does not love me." By consistently abandoning myself in order to be loved by others, I was fitting the definition pretty fucking perfectly. And I wasn't even sure I believed in karma. But karma is only there so we can learn from it. It's not there to trap us or to keep us in subservience to it. It's there to push us to free ourselves from the things that make us unhappy.

I had the keys to my redemption, if I was willing to take the responsibility to make another choice instead. And in saying "Fuck This", I was also saying that I was finished with living a life of Shit, where sacrificing myself was the only route to joy and where virtue was earned by strife. I was done making my heart smaller and my dreams lighter so that other people could stomach them. I was done allowing everyone else's definition of a good life to dictate my own. I was done putting power in someone else's hands, whether they were a hope, a reality, or a myth. I was ready to stop suffering, to stop hiding, to stop trying their way, and to give mine a chance. Because no matter what happened next, it would be better than whatever hell I had been accepting as my life.

Ultimately, in saying "Fuck This," I could embrace what felt perfect to me: following the joy wherever it took me. That is what my heart had been telling me all along, and not only did I silence it with my mind, but I also silenced it with other people's. And if that meant losing the religion of pain to do it, well then… with pleasure. My unicorn had a comfortable saddle.

Free Your Mind
Liz

As we've shared in the podcast, a basic spiritual under-standing is that we have four main bodies:

1. The physical: what we can see and touch in everyday life.

2. The mental: how we think and process our thoughts.

3. The emotional: what our feelings are.

4. The spiritual: how we connect to and experience our divinity.

Many spiritual teachers also discuss the higher, subtle bodies, and there are other terms and vocabulary around how we exist as spiritual beings. Frankly, I don't believe there's any reason to learn about those unless we have a burning desire to do so. Of course, there will always be a great deal we have yet to learn and master, but once we understand and distill the language of spirit and a few simple teachings, many other ideas and practices become irrelevant. Like mindfulness.

Mindfulness was an essential practice in a world of judgment and Separation because our bodies operated separately from one another. It was a spiritual concept intended to bridge the mental body with the spiritual one (not to be confused with meditation, a practice that connects all four bodies through the spiritual body, just as sex does through the physical one). But today, it's a way to bypass our discomfort in our physical reality by allowing us to ignore the underlying emotional issues that need to surface.

Mindfulness has become the spiritual middle ground. It enables us to influence our emotional state in any given moment, simply by reassuring us that all we are perceiving is merely a construct. It doesn't require subscribing to a particular faith, and there is no membership fee. All we need is to become aware of ourselves in relation to our environment and see how that self responds to it. But by giving our mental body too much control over our emotional and physical ones, it has become corrupted. And because it is especially adept at reminding us that everything is an illusion (so all we need to do is calm the fuck down and see life for what it is, which is a transitory state), it offers the fantasy that everything can be better tomorrow.

It's understandable that we have bought into it. We are experts at avoidance, we are professionals when it comes to denial, and we are specialists at distracting ourselves at every turn. We'll do whatever it takes to stem the tide of fear that threatens to overcome us at any moment. But with all the ongoing judgment, resulting shame, our karma, and our issues being flung up at us, we've imploded.

As much as we'd like to get back to a time when we

could make sense of everything, we're past the point of no return. Our world is disintegrating before our very eyes, along with many of our relationships, and we can't handle it. We've dabbled and delved into a variety of psycho-spiritual modalities and homeopathic remedies only to find temporary relief.

But it's all a big fat lie… All of it—from the mindfulness seminars to the paths to inner peace sold as a package weekend at a sunny resort. None of that is going to get us to our true healing. Like any other vice or habit, they're just plugging the holes we're experiencing—the holes that resulted from our karma—only offering a transient reprieve to keep us from really losing our Shit.

We've relied on the mental body to take care of us for so long that we're having to play catch-up with our other bodies, which are a mess. Amid this chaos, the mental body is shutting down. Even though we may buy into the illusion that we are in control of our lives and perspectives, we cannot rationalize our issues, no matter how much we wish to. If something needs to be addressed, it'll be in our faces until we open our eyes to it. But the longer we remain in denial and "mindfully" ignore our issues, the greater our suffering becomes.

Set U Free

To evolve and come into our divinity through our karma, we need our spiritual bodies, especially if we wish to evolve by leaps and bounds since our spiritual body gets us there faster than the others. That's because they are the connection to our souls and how we connect to our divinity. The more in touch we are with our divinity, the more we are able to create the life we desire for ourselves and those we love.

But we've never been able to connect to our divinity because we've been conditioned to surrender responsibility for our spiritual bodies. Historically, there would always be someone to come along and save us; or all we had was this life, so we may as well make the most of our time. Either way, we left our spiritual bodies behind.

There are a variety of meditation practices that enable full bodily connection (that is, all four bodies aligning to connect to a greater wisdom from within) and also allow for complete divine transcendence. When we allow our gaze to drift to our third eye and open up to our spiritual body, it allows us to connect to our souls.

Our souls are not what makes us divine, however. They serve as the vehicles to our Point of Essence, that very place of Oneness that allows for the most transcendent existence we could possibly experience. Since we are not yet at a place of complete Oneness in our world because we have yet to be fully at One with ourselves individually, we are afforded the mirrored experience, which in its purest form, can be totally transcendent.

What holds us back from our spiritual body, and hence our divinity, is our inability to face our emotions. And mindfulness can't get us there because in order to survive polarity, our mental body has labeled things as dangerous, wrong, or risky so we know what to avoid to prevent our emotional bodies from being overwhelmed. However, as our consciousness expands (not just the mind but all four bodies expanding simultaneously), we have had to confront everything that our minds have contained to bring our bodies into harmony. And we do not have words for all the hurt, pain, and destruction that our experiences have afflicted our emotional bodies. It's crippling to even imagine how we'd explain these emotions that so many of us would rather not.

The beauty of karma is that our issues are packaged quite neatly, allowing us to recognize the stories we've constructed to support our karmic themes. These themes reveal themselves in our relationships—with others, a particular institution, or our work—and inevitably, they point to our experience of not being *good enough*. But our mental bodies have developed coping mechanisms for our karma, AKA egos, that tell us we are *good enough* in order to keep us from having to deal with our issues. And meditation does not and cannot work if we bring the ego into it. It merely amplifies it.

We developed our egos as a protective barrier between us and the scary world. In a world of Separation, they're the part of us that works to be *good enough* in every scenario. They tell us that how we are doing in this life is based on two things: having more than others (for instance, lifestyle, money, career, and family) and feeling better than others (where we are on the happiness scale). All of these speak to the surface area of our lives and allow the ego to keep us in check while neglecting the welfare of our bodies.

Mindfulness has become the ego's version of meditation. It is the spiritual hack the ego has been waiting for because it allows the ego to stay intact while convincing us we're actually on the path to healing. It tells us we've found the key to inner peace and that the mind can unlock it for us. And if we dive into mindfulness with a distorted image of ourselves, guided by an ego that's resolved to save us from ourselves, we will come away not only unhealed but with an elevated ego that we may confuse for our divinity.

To be fair, it's not the fault of our mental bodies that we're in this predicament. We needed them to deal with polarity and the subsequent judgment, and they did the best they could. But it's not enough anymore. Our bodies cannot operate independently in Oneness consciousness. They are meant to function harmoniously. This means we have to align them with one another.

To have all four bodies in complete alignment means that they are functioning to their greatest capacity, given our personal limitations. We don't have to aim for incredible peak athleticism (physical), having zero anxiety or worry (mental), being happy all the time (emotional), or being in a constant state of bliss (spiritual). Rather, to be in alignment means doing the best we can as we work through our karma. It means finding the humility required to untangle ourselves from those parts of our lives that aren't working for us. It means being fearless and saying no to the things that don't serve us. Finally, it means that in the thick of it all, through all our issues and worries and fears and anxieties and griefs, there's the trust that our lives don't have to be as we've always believed them to be.

Bills, Bills, Bills
Liz

As the saying goes, the glass is either half empty or half full. And depending on how we perceive it speaks to our general disposition. Are we more optimistic or pessimistic? Do we choose to see what is there as opposed to what is not? Of course, there's never a right answer because both speak to a truth. Like Schrodinger's paradox, the glass is both half empty *and* half full. However, in the spiritual sense, the glass is neither half empty *nor* half full. Rather, it is filled with the potential of what is and what can be. Just because we don't see something doesn't mean that it's not there. It has merely yet to materialize in our physical realm.

When we work with the energy of Abundance, the concept is the same. Even though we may not recognize our Abundance in our everyday lives, it doesn't mean it's not there or that it cannot be brought into the material world. It merely takes our egos not attaching to any expectations or outcomes because we're not realizing our role in how to bring it forth into our reality. We alone are responsible for our Abundance. But until we really understand what it is and what keeps it at bay, we will not be able to experience Abundance in the fullest sense of the word.

Despite the theories, manifestos, and teachings regarding Abundance, there is only one absolute rule when it comes to Abundance (well two, but the second one is more of a principle): we are the creator of our lives, and only we can create the Abundance needed to shape them. Abundance is not bestowed upon us by anyone or anything. It's not a matter of luck (luck being a form of superstition that has everything to do with fear), and it is not about working hard and saving money because Abundance is not about having enough or an excess of money. (That's the second thing I mentioned above: Abundance has nothing to do with money.) Nor is it about perspective, that is, choosing to see what we have instead of what we don't and believing we will always have something. This has nothing to do with Abundance because it is not something that can be attained.

Abundance is an energy and therefore cannot be regarded as an object, nor can it be contained, as we are constantly creating it. But the more significance we attach to it, the less likely it will ever arrive at our feet— not because it's a form of punishment because we want something so badly, but because if we set an obstacle or barrier between us and Abundance, for example, fear or self-doubt, then it cannot reach us.

The more we make Abundance a specific goal, especially to relieve our fears or satiate our ego, as opposed to a by-product of a greater goal or desire we've set for ourselves, the more we will repel it. In order to work with any kind of benevolent energy, such as Abundance, we must first regard ourselves honestly. Are we capable of treating it responsibly? Will we respect it enough to allow it to flow? Do we carry a sense of lack in our hearts that will distort the energy?

For many, Abundance has been the elusive lover because we've been unable to answer these questions satisfactorily. We've been conditioned to believe that we're never far from losing everything or being wiped out while there's one percent of the population who have more than the rest. This belief that we exist within the state of all or nothing suspends us in an existence where we are either one step away from ultimate destruction or the sheer hopelessness of ever changing our personal circumstances.

Separation has kept us in fear for so long that most of us cannot envision a world where this has merely been a product of our twisted imaginations, that beneath the layers of inequity and fear, there's another reality waiting to emerge—one that allows Abundant energy to flow freely among us so that we can all enjoy it.

The only way for this to happen is for us to acknowledge that we've created our world. Most of us don't recognize that we are the architects of our reality—not only by how we perceive our realities but in acknowledging that we are our Creator.

We have been brought up to believe someone or something else created us. We've been taught that our existence is merely happenstance and that our lives, in the grand scheme of the universe, are specks of stardust. However, we are greater than these limiting beliefs. These limiting beliefs keep us small. They keep us in line. They keep us from exercising our will. They keep us in fear, and as a result, they keep us in lack. And so long as we remain in lack, we remain apart from Abundance. Only by acknowledging that we are the originators of our lives can we make the most of all the energy available to us in a new, expanded reality.

Abundance does not relate to money (because if we stopped using money, the energy would still exist); yet, given the economic structures of our world, it could be regarded in part as growing wealth. But it's not about everyone becoming millionaires or billionaires. Rather, it involves increasing their financial potential so that it has a knock-on effect around the world. It's not possible to create Abundance at the expense of others, however. Wealth gained by exploiting others isn't true Abundance. Instead, it is an excess of money stimulated by avarice, which is born from Separation. As Rhea once shared, Abundance is like a tap that is always on. Exploiting wealth, however, is like getting a cup of water from a filled bath without a tap. It is water; it came from somewhere, but it will eventually dry up.

As we continue to wake up to the lies we've willingly lived by to survive our fearful world, as we move into expanded consciousness, and as we find our legs on the shaky ground of a new, emerging reality, our tolerance for those who have accumulated money at others' expense will diminish. Part of enabling Abundance and tapping into its energy means not allowing others to have power over us. So, as power shifts from a single entity to a collective one (in that the more empowered we are individually, the more empowered we can be as a collective), we will see more wealth being poured into our world.

While some may find that their life path involves creating wealth through Abundance, others may find that wealth interferes with their larger goals and desires. Ultimately, it is no one's fate to only acquire financial wealth in their lifetime, just as it is no one's fate to die penniless. In Oneness consciousness, Abundance ensures that anything and everything is possible. As we venture away from polarity and into Oneness consciousness, our growth and our evolution will not involve lack or strife or struggle. We will grow without suffering, know love without having to experience its antithesis, and engage with our wisdom without interference.

Abundance is an essential component of Oneness consciousness. When we are connected to our inherent creator power, Abundance becomes an extension of that power. So, when we've been able to harness Abundance for ourselves, it means that we've been able to release ourselves from the fear that keeps us tied to Separation. And when we are no longer living in Separation, and when we've connected to the greater collective Oneness that our internal Oneness enables, Abundance is ours to play with.

She Works Hard for the Money

We are now just seeing the inklings of Abundance creation in our younger generations. Generation Z is the first to be wholly and completely connected to this energy. This is because, before them, there was still too much Separation and strife to make Oneness possible. Yet as Oneness consciousness emerged (the potential for which bloomed under the feet of these young ones), the more we saw the first wave of true Abundance entering our world. And since they are the most connected to Oneness of any generation before them, in that they are not burdened by the weight of karma as previous ones, they have been able to make the most of Abundance in ways we had not realized were imaginable.

Abundance isn't just reserved for Gen Zers though. It's available to everyone who has done the work to expand their consciousness. It's meant to be experienced by each and every person in every corner of this world. Abundance is accessible to everyone who lives beyond the world of excess, lack, Separation, and fear. In the end, Abundance is a choice, and choosing it means lifting the curse that Separation brings, which is one of limiting self-belief.

If it's one thing Gen Zers do not have, it's limiting self-belief. It's almost shocking to older generations to witness the way these young ones simultaneously upend expectations around spending and accumulating wealth while championing social freedoms. The reason they seem so unpredictable is that they are not tied to the narrative around polarity and Separation, or avarice versus sacrifice. Instead, they are making up their own narratives as they go.

They are not stuck in the old paradigm of enslaving themselves to a system to make money in order to afford a house, car, or family—only to retire and then die. Rather, they operate within the NOW, which tells us the only thing that matters is the NOW, which means they will tend to what demands their attention NOW and shift to the next thing once a goal is accomplished. Underpinning all of this is Abundance energy, which enables us to live in the NOW without worry over the future or regret over the past. It means that we already have all we need, and should we require anything else, Abundance will provide it.

Abundance is the larger, encompassing energy that contains the potential for all that is possible to be experienced on our Earth plane in this lifetime. And it's free to use so long as we are free from all the constructs and constraints that have kept us believing in our Separation. All we need to do is look at our younger generation as examples; to see how confidently they stride through life, knowing their place in it, fighting for a future we feared wasn't possible. They do this knowing Abundance is there to support them. All we need is to believe it, too.

Takin' Care Of Business
Rhea

It wasn't until I started working that I learnt that often our relationship with money is a smokescreen for far bigger issues. Because behind the apparent safety is lack, and behind that structure is fear. And underneath it all, almost everyone is fucking miserable.

Like many, I assumed that I had to work hard, via an established career, and that it would all be enough. I could make enough money to buy anything I wanted and have a snazzy business title that I could whip out at dinner parties and casual networking events. So I followed the steps to create exactly that. University graduation followed by law school graduation followed by working at a law firm; I was doing everything that was expected of me, but there was a catch: I was suffering for my safety, suffering for my security, and suffering to follow the path that I believed I had to follow. I didn't dare to dream that my joy could also be my purpose. Instead, I told myself that if this was what I was meant to do, then I would do it or die trying.

Although, when it became my reality (rather than just a series of hypothetical steps), it turned out that I couldn't.

I felt trapped, anxious, and powerless. Sunday evenings were the worst nights of the week, and I was so miserable that I forgot to breathe. I wanted to make it bearable, but my body wouldn't let me. Eventually, I could not take the pressure of trying to fit in anymore and I broke. The fear of other people's judgment was overshadowed by the fear of losing my mind. In my first "Fuck This," I realized that no matter how much financial security I had, I was so far away from my own wants and needs that peace would always elude me.

But somehow, when at rock bottom, I was liberated. I knew I couldn't do it anymore—that anything was better than this.

The irony is that when we stop doing what we really don't want to be doing, whilst it frees us up to do what we actually want, we're not usually ready for the freedom we've been handed. I wasn't ready to live this abundant life that Liz describes; I didn't know what living in the NOW was, and I definitely didn't think that I had some kind of spiritual safety net that would catch me. I also wasn't ready for Oneness consciousness, nor did I even know that it was a thing.

But I was ready to stop being miserable—and because I was young enough to not have my work ethic entirely corrupted by Separation, I wasn't focusing on all the ways it could go wrong but how it could work out in my favor. My naiveté allowed me to believe that I could create a working life that suited me from the heart, rather than one that involved losing it. And even though it was difficult to convince other people to see it my way, I wanted it enough that I didn't care. I readily accepted that they would disagree with me until they didn't, that they would make their own judgments that had nothing to do with me and everything to do with their expectations of me. I was going to follow my excitement and see where it would lead.

And it worked. I wasn't earning millions, and it often looked like I was making unhinged decisions (like agreeing to run a domestic violence charity with a girl whom I had a one-hour lunch with or starting a podcast with a lady who hears voices in her head). But when I listened to my heart, I didn't just find that I landed on my feet, I landed somewhere new that allowed me to achieve my goals, until I was ready to move on to the next one.

I woke up every morning and felt a sense of calm purpose which I carried with me throughout my day. Sunday evenings went from being the dreaded beginning of another week to just another evening. I looked forward to what I was doing, barely noticing how hard I was working. Money and financial security were replaced with joy and meaning, and I allowed myself to live a life I could be proud of. I was creating the work life I wanted, not what someone else expected of me, and my confidence and trust grew with every new choice.

Yes, I could have become a lawyer. I could have worked a 9 to 5 every day (well, more like 9 to midnight because those hours can be long). I could have had enough money under the bed to buy the right house, buy the right things, and buy the right life. I could have pretended to have it all. But I would have been denying the trust I had in my heart, the faith that said I was here for more than sacrifice, the knowing that I could create more than security, and the hope that life could be even more than I could imagine at that moment.

Despite how it appeared on the surface, I never forgot the importance of having an income in order to survive. I was aware of how I spent, and I dug into the boundless energy that was helping me to achieve my dreams. Frankly, the alternative wasn't an alternative for me. It wasn't being rebellious for rebellion's sake; it was the understanding that I would only truly be successful if I defined what my success meant. That was worth the risk of not knowing all the answers.

In Chapter Seventeen, I spoke about how I wanted to choose something other than the religion of sacrifice. But I wasn't sure how to do it or what it would lead to. How silly. Turns out that I had been doing it with my career since 2008, and I had all the answers that I had been looking for all along. I had seen that following the joy not only meant finding more joy but also eventually love. I knew what it meant to be fearless, and I knew it would work out, even if it wasn't how I thought it would. That trust allowed me to take risks based on feelings, and those risks only ever ended up in my highest good because they allowed me to not only fulfill my dreams but to create new ones and fulfill them, too. I knew how to choose differently, but I was only applying that to one aspect of my life rather than all of it.

Maybe it wasn't a coincidence that it was the only aspect of my life where everything seemed to work out.

Good Girl Gone Bad
Rhea

For most of my life, I thought I needed to be a good girl. I believed that was the only way to achieve my goals, and I controlled everything as much as possible to create that illusion. As such, I searched for perfection, allowing other people's descriptions of what a good girl was to dictate my behavior.

I didn't realize that in believing that my actions could control how someone else felt about me; I was totally forgetting that they were usually going to see me through the lens of how they saw themselves. They were always going to wind up needing me in the ways they felt they were lacking, and they were only going to love me as much as they had the capacity and willingness to love. I was also forgetting that no matter what I did, I could never control myself enough to become an entirely different person.

So I would panic that time was running out; rehashing conversations, re-examining memories, and replaying my behavior to the point where I nearly drove myself mad. Most people had met their significant others at 30, or they were younger than me and seemed to have figured out their lives. Somehow, they hit every milestone at the right time with the right person in the right way, when I was still figuring out the right approach.

Time was my adversary, and the ticking clock was leading me to my demise. I was stuck waiting for my life to begin whilst also trying to be punctual. But even when it came to gym classes, social engagements, work meetings, or even dates, something always happened that meant I was left rushing, stressing, screaming, and eventually apologizing for being late.

I couldn't see all that I had because I was too busy focusing on what I still hadn't achieved. I couldn't see the potential of the future because I was too busy focusing on the pain of the past. And I couldn't live in the moment because I was scared the next one would wipe me out—all the while missing the moments that counted.

To be fair, I started at a disadvantage. I had the emotional range of a teenager and the fear of an older woman with everything to lose. I didn't believe I had time to try another way, and it wasn't worth the risk. I was time's prisoner, and I allowed it to keep me from my freedom because I was limiting my experiences in terms of *what* a good girl did and *when* a good girl earned as a result. That was always my double-edged relationship and what was mirrored in every other relationship I had; who I really was versus who I was settling to be, for the "should" and the "should happen next."

When I was sacrificing my happiness to stay in a relationship that wasn't working, when I was curating my dating profile to showcase my attractive qualities, when I was denying my personality or feelings, when I bought into the lie that we are all here to suffer, and when I believed that we don't get to live life on our own terms—those beliefs were all based on fears that my ego was protecting me from. I couldn't be sure that being myself, and listening to myself, would work out in my favor.

But in indulging those fears and letting my ego take the reins, I allowed them to become my reality instead, never giving myself the opportunity to find out if they were true or whether they were simply a construction that I forced myself to believe in order to survive.

Except it was actually the disconnect between who I was and who I thought I needed to be that tore me apart. And it was my insistence on maintaining it, whilst expecting certain results, that separated me from who I really was. In avoiding what I believed was a fate akin to death, I was slowly killing my will to live.

Knockin' On Heaven's Door

I am not qualified to talk about what happens to us after we die, but I do know what it's like to live with death, how losing a loved one hurts more than anything, and how that grief follows us every day and is triggered in the most unexpected ways. I know how a moment can change everything, and I know what it's like to be part of a club where the price of entry feels like a part of our hearts.

Yet, whether or not we have lost someone, death still affects our lives every day. Because in our own way, we are all constantly trying to out-think, out-pray, out-feel, and out-live it, whilst comparing ourselves to everyone else who is just doing the same thing. Maybe we monitor what we put into our bodies with the zeal of a *fitfluencer* or binge on fast food because of YOLO. Maybe we refuse to be open or put ourselves in situations where we end up pouring our hearts out. Maybe we pray to be absolved of our sins or rationalize that there is no life after death, anyway. Maybe we follow all the rules to stay alive or self-sabotage because we don't feel like we deserve our desires. Maybe we fear the end of anything because it could be the end of everything, too. Regardless of how we deal with it, death is the incontrovertible fact of life that we all cannot escape, and our world of polarity, black and white, good and bad, right and wrong, is confirmed by the polarity of life and death.

But I could never truly live if I kept running away from death, whilst wondering if I was running out of time to start living or pretending that it didn't exist. Doing so would only ensure that I remained exactly where I didn't want to be: scared and impotent to create a life that I actually wanted. That's why in saying "Fuck This" and making a different choice, I actually learnt what it meant to shift my reality. When I questioned my stories, pushed myself to take risks, and gave myself permission to listen to what I actually wanted to do, I found out what the consequences actually were. In other words, I just did whatever I wanted whenever I wanted, and to my surprise, it often worked out.

Turns out that all the stories that I had told myself, and the potential pitfalls I had been avoiding weren't pitfalls at all; they were ways in which I could discover who I actually was and what I wanted my life to look like. It almost didn't matter what happened next (as in making a different choice that wasn't confined to the judgments of others), I allowed my possibilities to expand, and I allowed myself to expand with them. In focusing on myself rather than on someone else's arbitrary milestones, I was finally working with time rather than against it, simply because I was creating my own timeline.

Moreover, every time I followed my heart, I became someone ever so slightly different because of the experience that followed. Every layer uncovered a new fear, a hidden expectation, and ultimately, a new perspective. Every change destroyed the version of me who existed before and allowed a new, more connected one to step into its place.

I already knew there was life after death because I had been dying in every lesson, in every choice, and in every moment where I followed my heart. To grow and change, I had to let the small parts of me that were holding me back from my freedom die. In fact, I had lived far more lives than I had appreciated, simply because every time I died, I was also becoming more me. Through death, I hadn't just been growing up and learning to embrace who I really was, I had also been transcending my ego's doubts that were telling me it wasn't possible.

When I allowed myself to be honest, the person who erected that wall crumbled with it. When I allowed myself to be courageous, I learnt that I was far more capable than I had previously envisaged. When I gleaned a new skill, I learnt that I could expand beyond my perceived limitations. I was living proof that death wasn't the end; it was a necessary part of growth and it was never the final destination. Death wasn't the end at all, it was the beginning.

Interestingly, my initial fear was right: the person who didn't believe they were *good enough* to be themselves was going to die before experiencing anything different. Time was running out on her fears and her excuses. But that person wasn't me, she was just a version of me. And the more I followed my heart instead of the shell I created to keep me safe, the more my light slipped through those cracks until me expressing my light was all that remained.

My light was creating a life that I never thought was possible. By living my life by choice and my timeline, regardless of my ego's perceived consequences, I kept expanding that light whilst also turning my fear into trust. This brought me closer to the truth: I had always been *good enough* to know love, and I didn't need to be a good girl to find it.

Being scared of endings, because it was safer to stay put, rather than taking a chance on something different, stopped me from seeing what would come next. Being scared of death never allowed me to live. But the past was just my perspective, and the future would always be unknown, regardless of my expectations. No matter what I tried to control, the only constant had been, and would continue to be, growth and change in unexpected ways.

And fuck me, it was a lot more joyful living on my own terms than living as a good girl, anyway. I finally wasn't splitting myself in return for someone else's acceptance whilst dismissing my own. Because the more I listened to myself, the more I learnt that love was present in all the moments when I was true to myself, mistakes, or otherwise. As long as I chose myself first, there was never a change that would mean I would lose it.

Death was merely the link between one existence and another, pushing me forward to more joy and happiness than I ever thought possible. It was how I gave myself a real chance at a life I desired, not what someone else desired of me. It was how I found out that I was so much more than my fears allowed me to believe. It was also how I learnt that I was so much bigger than anything I thought could imprison me.

Turns out, without the *good* to hold me back, I was *enough*. The unknown wasn't scary after all, it was limitless. But only by having the courage to allow myself to die and die again, could I ever be limitless in it.

Free Fallin'
Rhea

The Law of Attraction (AKA manifestation) is a clear concept: the universe will provide us with what we believe we deserve or, falling short of that, what we believe we are owed. Therefore, if we want to receive or experience different things, we have to believe we can have them. The understanding is that the ability itself doesn't come from the present mind but from our subconscious: the part of our mind that's hidden, where all our actions and reactions stem from. In rewiring our subconscious mind, we can raise our vibration to match what we believe we want or need, and in setting the intention, we put things in motion. Even if we're not yet at the optimal vibrational level, the universe will provide us with lessons and experiences to help us get there.

Now, this approach makes sense in a lot of ways because, on some level, this type of work is just logic (with a little energetic healing thrown in for good measure). The more we believe we are worthy of something, the less willing we are to settle. The more we believe in the existence of what we are looking for, the less likely we are to accept an imitation. So, in holding true to our wants, we eventually realize them in our physical world. And, as a bonus point, we can also start to believe in the universe too. It's the seemingly magic wand that works in the real world.

But before you get excited, manifestation requires effort and sacrifice. We need to be clear on what we want, including all the minute details of the thing, person, or job we are seeking. (For those who prefer to visualize #dreamlife, you can design a vision board.) We then have to unpick the doubts and stories about why we don't deserve them, acknowledge that those beliefs are holding us back, and journal or meditate on our issues whilst attempting to show they don't govern our decisions. We have to prove that we are serious after all, and what better way to do that than to self-flagellate whilst convincing ourselves that deep down we were deserving the whole time?

Yet, all of this "critical thinking" and "mental self-evaluation" is key to manifestation. Because to earn the prize, we have to pass the tests that show we aren't willing to settle for anything less. This may include walking away from a potential mate who doesn't tick all of our boxes, turning down a job that requires a bit too much hard work, or getting comfortable spending money despite an overdraft larger than the national debt of a developing country. However, if we can't navigate these tests by indulging in the wrong person, role, or experience for too long, then we may have to wait until the right one comes along. It's not to say that it's never coming. We just need to improve ourselves, our worthiness, our vibration, or our journaling skills (and maybe throw in some affirmations for good measure).

Of course, I bought into the manifestation concept hook, line, and sinker. Finally, there was evidence that my suspicions were correct. I wasn't *good enough* to get what I wanted, but in working harder on myself, the universe would reward me for surrendering to the idea that I wasn't *good enough* and repenting for it. I also saw it working for other people, and I was very good at using other people's solutions for my problems. They had the answers, and I wanted some quick fixes. Most importantly, manifestation triggered every point on my "if only I was *good enough*" checklist:

✓ Want what other people tell you to want.

✓ Follow the rules.

✓ Do lots of work to prove you are worthy.

✓ Get ready for tests to illustrate that worthiness.

✓ Make the right decisions to get your prize.

✓ Understand that if you don't get it, then something is wrong with you, so just work harder *(super check here)*.

And it worked (a little). Problem was, it was also tiring and, frankly, a massive headfuck. When crafting my wants and working through my stories, I was doing so with the zeal of a sprinter running a marathon. In surrounding myself with all the ways in which I wasn't *good enough,* I made it the only thing that I experienced. I kept myself as a constant work in progress, and I became so scared to make a mistake that it crippled me. It wasn't just another person who would punish me for still thinking that I was not *good enough,* it was the universe.

None of my old habits were going anywhere. They were just being repackaged and repurposed with the universe as the excuse for why I still believed my fears over believing in myself. Except in trying to outrun my fears, I never questioned why I had put any of the things on my list in the first place. So whilst checking things off may have made me feel good in the short term, I wasn't any more satisfied than before I started. In fact, I was often settling for what I thought was achievable, which wasn't very much considering how often I meditated on the belief that I was not *good enough.*

Without realizing it, my penchant for toxic relationships was transferred onto manifestation. (Spoiler alert: I did so because I hadn't actually dealt with my penchant for toxic relationships despite all my journaling about them.) And nothing I tried to manifest brought me closer to love and freedom. It kept me trapped in my ego's idea of love and freedom—whilst consistently reaffirming that I wasn't *good enough* to get it.

Turns out the only thing I was really good at manifesting was the reasons for which I wasn't *good enough* to manifest anything at all. So, after another experience where everything had been done by the book but the universe had still failed to provide, I was left with a list with only one point: Fuck you, Universe.

Learn to Fly

When we do what we think we should, rather than what we want, we are not vanquishing our fears. We are moving them into the next experience instead. And whether or not it looks exactly the same, our experience of it will be, simply because we cannot outrun the feeling of not being *good enough*.

If we worry we will always be abandoned, we look for ways in which it will happen whilst looking to others to reassure us otherwise. If we think we always have to settle, we naturally settle for what we think we can have whilst trying to convince ourselves that we aren't settling at all. Or if we fear we are unlovable, we create toxic relationships with everything and everyone in our lives, including the universe.

Now, this isn't meant to be a cautionary tale. I'm merely stating that our fears are irrational and our unresolved Shit always follows us around, no matter how hard we try to contain it. And whilst that makes karma seem like an inescapable bitch, it's actually showing us how it is a helpful one. After trying everything else, we eventually learn that no matter what we do, nothing outside of us can convince us we are lovable, worthy, deserving, good, perfect, whole, and that we matter. Only we can.

Learning about how I believed I wasn't *good enough* was never going to be a surprise, so in littering my home with list after list of things I wanted but feared I couldn't have, I ensured I remained lacking. I kept my world confined to a narrow view where I needed to experience my checklist how I'd written it, ensuring that I was perpetually disappointed. Therefore, in applying the manifestation rules to my Shitty situations, I kept myself trapped in them.

When I walked away from an experience before I was ready (surreptitiously passing my tests), I was actually compounding the fear that I wasn't *good enough* to decide for myself whether I needed to walk away. When I prioritized external validation, or what I thought would eventually lead to external validation, I reinforced that my feelings were less important than how it looked like I felt. When I forced myself to stay between the rigid lines I had set for myself, I kept running into the same person with a different face or the same situation in a different setting.

But when I said "Fuck you, Universe," what I was actually saying was "Fuck This." I was acknowledging that I was sick of my Shit, and if the Law of Attraction was only going to attract what I didn't want, then I was sick of it too. I realized that throughout this entire process, by consistently giving my energy to a reality where I was miserable unless I was compliant, I was making it real. Because the more I feared I wasn't *good enough* and tried to prove otherwise, the more I experienced it (it's the Law of Attraction, after all).

It's not that the Law of Attraction doesn't work. But unless we get rid of our karma, it will be a whole lot of karmic attraction rather than anything else. I can tell you from personal experience that I was able to "manifest" a whole lot of something into my world. But I was also left with nothing because I was cycling through my fears, constantly worrying that my negative thoughts would lead to negative experiences, and creating scenarios to reinforce my fears.

Of course I was manifesting Shitty situations. I was drowning in my Shit, and the Law of Attraction was jumping on my karmic bandwagon and doubling down on the Shit I kept attracting until I dealt with it. But when we use manifestation to save us or discredit our fears, we are actually reinforcing them and allowing our Shit to dictate our experiences.

Looking to others to give us the tools to use it in the first place shows how little we understand its potential and our own. Yet, what underpins manifestation, and why so many believe it works, is because they actually believe it. However, in trying to hack the system rather than honoring it, we have narrowed our possibilities and our power. In using manifestation to get out of our Shit, we unwittingly pile on more, looping through our powerlessness without realizing how powerful we really are.

That is how manifestation has abused the Law of Attraction and why it's so damn limiting. Until we understand that our lives have more meaning than proving our worth by passing some arbitrary test of will, we will keep failing. Until we understand that the only way to raise our vibration is to embrace how fucking great we are, regardless of what we say, do, or think, or how we act, we will keep searching for validation outside of ourselves. And until we understand that no one else can tell us we are *good enough*, we'll never figure out what we actually want.

But I wanted to figure it out. I was done waiting for someone or something else to deliver the life that I desperately craved. If I wanted something different, I needed to be okay with making mistakes. My life couldn't be focused on defending myself from what could go wrong. It had to be about trusting that things could go right.

I couldn't judge my experiences whilst being in the middle of them, and I couldn't see where they'd lead even if I wanted to (despite having a gifted psychic as my work wife). Because if I could believe in myself with my entire being, I could also create a whole other reality that fundamentally worked for me.

For example, my entire dating life, as evidenced at the start of this book, was an epic Shitshow. In every single chapter, there was a plethora of reasons why I should have walked away at the start, rather than sticking around and discovering why they failed to meet the criteria on my list. But in following my curiosity and compulsion to keep going, I allowed myself to have new experiences and learn something new about myself, whilst experiencing my entire karmic undoing process.

Naturally, I could have followed the manifestation handbook, cut each one off because it wasn't 100%, and patted myself on the back for passing another test. I could have turned to my friends and received many accolades for being clear on what I wanted and not accepting anything less. But if I had walked away when I didn't want to, I would have missed every seminal lesson that showed me *why* I was attracting those people and *what* I wanted to do about it. I would have turned away from the mirror in search of a better angle that would never come. My outlook wouldn't have changed enough to change my life. But in listening to myself instead of the manifestation handbook, I got out of my karma, which was skewing my world. I also learnt that none of the things on my list actually mattered. It had never been about the guy who looked right on paper, it was about the one who felt right, or in whose presence I could be myself without pretense or explanation.

By throwing out the checklists in exchange for real connection, dismissing other people's rules in exchange for having an open mind, and choosing to be present instead of being preoccupied with the future, I created what I really wanted. I also learnt what would carry me through to the end of my karmic story and beyond— that when we give ourselves permission to live our lives according to our own rules, we can manifest whatever the fuck we want. And once we can understand how powerful we really are, we won't even need the Law of Attraction to do it for us.

La Vie en rose
Liz

If there was ever a blanket solution to all our negativity, cynicism, pessimism, and general bad moods, gratitude would be it. It's the natural mood lifter, attitude shifter, and game changer for spiritual lite practitioners. This is effectively the Law of Attraction at work, within its limits dictated by our karmic experiences. By appreciating everything we encounter, and expressing gratitude for those things we have or can experience, we see all the good things about our lives (even things that hurt but have made us stronger). Those who practice gratitude regularly believe it positively transforms our lives by focusing on the positive aspects of our reality, which creates space for more positivity to arise.

That's why we don't even have to be a Pollyanna to be grateful. We can simply train our brains to recognize those things we should appreciate: the sun (because, you know, vitamin D), the clouds (because, you know, skin cancer), the rain (because flowers and trees need water), and so on. It doesn't even matter if we have a glass-half-empty perspective because either way, life provides a host of learning opportunities to make us better people—even if they hurt like a motherfucker (so we can be #grateful for our karma too). All we need to do is look for the silver lining.

However, much like mindfulness, the gratitude practice is merely putting the proverbial cart before the horse. It pushes us to run before we can even stand. It asks us to fake it until we make it, with the assumption that if we can will it hard enough, good things will come. And as potent as gratitude can be, it's even more harmful than mindfulness because it uses the mental body to deny our honest emotions (mindfulness likes to control our emotions; gratitude pushes them away like a spiritual anti-depressant).

So we lean on pithy sayings to remind us that for every good, there is bad; for every storm, there's a rainbow; for every joy, there comes loss; and that misery is the inevitable precursor to happiness because it was always a blessing in disguise. We believe that our suffering leads to redemption, since for every misfortune, something better awaits us around the corner. We have all become martyrs, waiting for the dawn to follow the darkest hour. But while pain can lead to some profound lessons, we diminish the experience by thanking it away.

As a result, gratitude has become a crutch for our victimhood. For too long, we have been unable to acknowledge our miserable realities because we've been conditioned to believe we are powerless to change them. To make the most of "what we're given," we convince ourselves we're better off acknowledging the emotions that help us get through the day and denying the ones that frustrate us. It's understandable. Of course, life could be worse. Lifetime after lifetime of pain and suffering taught us that. Stories of war, famine, violence, and widespread systemic abuse within institutions teach us that we're never far away from our destruction. What's more, it hasn't been long since we've woken up to our own detrimental behaviors—personal and societal.

But the more aware we become of how terrible life really is, the more we scramble to make sense of it all without fully understanding the root causes. We join movements, scream into echo chambers, and get on our soapboxes about issues that we've willfully ignored because they're either too big or seemingly impossible to fix. Rather than allowing our wisdom and understanding to catch up to us, we react and plug holes to stem the tide of our fears to prevent them from overwhelming us—all the while being told by well-meaning spiritual teachers that showing gratitude is the way through.

Gratitude

As children, we know we are *good enough* until our life experiences tell us otherwise. It could be as simple as a personal failure over something that mattered deeply to us, an encounter with a controlling parent, or a relationship with a narcissist. For my son, it was with a bully. He'd endured being pushed down stairs, tripped, and physically assaulted for well over a year. But to ameliorate the no-win situation, he was told by his teacher that he should appreciate that he doesn't come from the same circumstances as his bully.

If my son had listened to his teacher, perhaps he would have pitied his bully instead of standing up to him. But pitying his bully wouldn't have improved anything in the long term. If nothing else, it would've shifted the power dynamic in favor of the bully because that's what gratitude does. In acknowledging that we are not responsible for the things happening outside our sphere of influence, the power moves even further away from us. And when we cease to be in our power, we begin to live in shame.

Shame is a tough beast to take on because it runs against our core truth, that we are *good enough*. When we face the idea that we are not, it creates a dissonance so great that it diminishes our divinity or personal power. We think that maybe that person is right. Maybe we're not as special or beautiful as we believed. And the more we sit with this dissonance, the more shame can take over, until we wind up in a spiral that can last years. It becomes the nagging voice that whispers we'll never finish or things will never really change. It echoes the constant reminder that not only are we not *good enough*, but we *Will never Be Good Enough*.

Even if we try to heal the wounds of our karmic themes, and work through our issues around feeling not *good enough* (unlovable, not worthy, nothing, undeserving, evil, imperfect, or broken), shame will tell us that although we may feel a bit better about ourselves and that our story is over, we're really not finished at all—thus sticking us in a loop that echoes our karmic theme, even if the theme itself has ended.

I Will never Be Good Enough is the root of our powerlessness. No matter what we do to improve ourselves, the perceived inevitability of pain or suffering means we can never fully escape our story. But even if we can see the absolute truth of it all, the fear of consequences—of things getting worse either by leaving a toxic relationship or a job that kills our souls—keeps us locked in our own demise. As a result, we remain in this purgatory, making the best out of our prison cells by dressing them up and feeling #blessed that things aren't worse. We look at the sunlight through the small window and appreciate that we get any light at all, ignoring the clues that we're really just imprisoned in our own hell.

Instead of dealing with our emotions, we have developed a coping mechanism for our suffering and powerlessness and called it gratitude.

Gratitude is our emotional prison. It keeps us on the emotional spectrum of just *good enough* to ensure we don't teeter over either end, and it reminds us what we have is enough. But it's not enough. It was only enough when we believed others could rob us of our power. It was only enough when we believed we didn't have the power to exercise our choices. It was only enough when we didn't have the power to change anything.

Thank U, Next

Polarity and Separation ensure that we are either on the side of wealth or lack, right or wrong, strong or weak. If someone is in power, then others are not, and therefore to survive, we must surrender what little power we have to a governing body, financial system, religion, or even a new-age belief system. But all the energy we spend writing in our gratitude journals, praying for things to get better, surrendering to the universe, having our astrological forecasts done, or getting into Twitter fights over failing political systems and policies is being wasted. They are merely distractions that keep us from dealing with the shame and disappointment of having lived in such a powerless state for so long.

It's painful to acknowledge that we've opted time and again for stories that have kept us enslaved to systems, jobs, debt, poverty, and relationships at the expense of our power. So when we exercise what little agency we have and nothing works, we blame others for our failure, further trapping us in our shame. But the fear of the fallout that could arise if we confronted our shame keeps us dependent on others to act on our behalf, and we miss the fact that if we want to be truly free from our pasts, we can no longer look to others to save us. Even those with the best intentions cannot help us because it keeps us in our victimhood and impotence. And so long as we need someone to come along and save us, we never realize that we are powerful enough to save ourselves.

But we don't wake up one day, decide we're done being powerless, and immediately change our lives for the better. Waking up and changing our lives is an internal process that takes time and persistence (Rhea will attest to that). That's where karma comes in. All of those challenging moments show us where we have been giving away our power. Karma gives us opportunity after opportunity to exercise our power by discovering that actually, maybe, we can be more powerful than life led us to believe. Except, often, because we haven't had much practice, or because our lives are set up in a way that exercising our power is nearly impossible, we usually give up after one setback. We turn our disappointments into self-fulfilling prophecies and vow to keep our heads down and just make the best of it (because, of course, it could always be worse).

Yet, worse comes when we ignore our issues and allow them to fester until they seep into other areas of our lives, infecting everything we experience. Karma ensures that no matter how hard we try, something else will grab our attention. This pushes us into our shame spirals and the belief that nothing will get better.

But it can and does get better. First, we need to utter Rhea's favorite phrase, "Fuck This." Then we need to acknowledge our issue. This is the toughest part because we have to face that we've let ourselves down more times than we'd like to count, but we can't get better if we don't know the root of our dis-ease (that is, not at ease; get it?). The key to understanding how and why we've let ourselves down is compassion. Because when we hold ourselves in compassion, we stop judging or condemning ourselves for our hurts, and we no longer have to shroud ourselves in shame.

Compassion and forgiveness are not new concepts in spiritual healing. However, so often we're taught that we must forgive others for hurting us and have empathy for those who don't know better. Yet compassion isn't kindness. It isn't turning the other cheek, seeing things through someone else's viewpoint, or being neighborly (highly overrated, given some of the neighbors I've had).

Compassion is being in step with others. It means that even if we have not experienced what they have, we can understand them—not because we empathize or sympathize but because their words and actions reveal where they are in their karmic evolution.

To *bring* ourselves into compassion, that is, to be in step with ourselves, is to embrace our pain. To *have* compassion for ourselves means to forgive ourselves for allowing that situation to play out in a way that hurt us or damaged our faith. To *live in* compassion means accepting that while our Shit could've happened some other way, it didn't; and while there's no changing the past, we are the only ones who can write what comes next.

Compassion demands responsibility and tolerance; to take responsibility for our choices and show tolerance to others who need the time and opportunity to do the same, without judgment or shame. But we cannot know what it means to be in step with others until we are in step with ourselves. And we cannot be in step with ourselves if we regard ourselves as victims.

Forgiveness isn't about accepting the hurt that someone has inflicted. Rather, it demands that we own our role in the story—that in choosing to be a part of this karmic story, we accept we are not anyone's victim, least of all our own victim. This is often the most difficult to understand because we presume that if we're really choosing what happens in our lives, then we would choose only the good things like having enough money, a great career, or fulfilling relationships. But the basic tenets of karma teach that we are rarely born into fortune and die satisfied. Rather, until we understand how powerful we are, we won't be able to do what we came here to do, which is to grow and evolve. And we do this not by navel-gazing or making sense of our suffering until we're dizzy, but by raising our consciousness. That is the beauty of karma; it doesn't allow us to skate through life. Instead, it paves the way for the joy we knew was possible before we became buried under the weight of our not *good enough* stories.

None of us are immune to karma. Shit has happened to each and every one of us. So we must accept that we are responsible for healing our wounds before we create a new experience for ourselves. But we don't need to be grateful for our Shit. We merely need to make our peace with it so we can realize our greatest state of being in this lifetime.

And when we can really heal our Shit, gratitude becomes a given, not a practice.

Let It Go
Rhea

When I was ready to heal, letting go was the answer to my prayers. For as long as I could remember, I'd been practicing a concept that told me my Shit was just circumstance, not who I really was. Letting go simply reinforced it. It assured me that all I had to do was recognize that I was not my pain or my stories and become a totally new person simply by telling myself that I hadn't been hurt in the first place.

Letting go also closed the loophole that I hadn't quite figured out because according to those who applied it regularly, if it didn't work (which appeared to involve taking a deep breath and saying "let it go" repeatedly), I could take it one step further. I could brush off my icky past experiences as misguided perceptions rather than true life experiences, tell myself it didn't happen as I experienced it, and get a gold star for my growth and evolution.

I threw all my energy into letting go, just like every other life hack that allowed me to circumvent my growth by pretending that I'd already grown up. Whenever I encountered an obstacle, a roadblock, a red flag, or an uncomfortable situation, I told myself to let it go. I never asked myself where my Shit really ended up, nor did I question whether it was actually freeing me from pain. I didn't care. Letting go taught me that if I ignored my Shit enough, it would either miraculously heal or it would simply cease to exist in my reality. Although, I wasn't too concerned, since I told myself I wouldn't allow the same Shit to happen again. I was older now, and I could safely assume that I was wiser too.

Problem was, although I could see that my life may have looked (marginally) different, I didn't feel it. I reasoned that I'd become so used to preparing for the worst that to shift my perspective overnight was impossible, although deep down I still doubted whether letting everything go was working. I was still haunted by my history and tainted by my Shit, believing that I was one experience or misstep away from slipping back to where I started. And to make it worse, my Shit kept showing up—whether it was in reality or the little voice in my head telling me to watch out and overthink before I jumped. It was frustrating and, frankly, a little embarrassing to admit because as much as I wanted to let go of those memories and the pain, for some reason, I couldn't.

My heart felt open but also traumatized by all the disappointments and betrayals from my past. My physical body was functioning but fracturing from the strain of my neglect. My mind was processing, but it was so exhausted that it hurt to think. And my spirit? Well, it couldn't let go of the past, no matter how much I forced it.

If there's one thing the past twenty-three chapters have emphasized, it's that our external world reflects our internal one. Our Shit shows up in big and small ways until we've made our peace with it. That means to truly let go of anything is to really, and I mean really, master that issue and eliminate all the fears around it. It requires learning every lesson around the issue so that it doesn't inform our present or perceived future (which is why Liz explains in Chapter One how letting go is actually just living consciously, without fear).

But I wouldn't have been able to master anything while pretending that it had never happened, or had only happened in a way that I could stomach. All I would master was a coping mechanism disguised as a spiritual hack, whilst unknowingly acting and reacting to past hurts and wondering why they were always so present. Sure, on the surface, it seemed easier to believe that I wasn't the person who had those Shitty experiences. Except, no matter what I tried to let go of, and how I tried to let it go, I could never fully let go of the girl and her string of disappointments.

To accept a new reality, I needed to completely own the reality I had lived in before. By judging the past version of me, I was holding on tighter to everything I wanted to let go of. I trapped myself in my story of not being *good enough* by telling myself that my feelings weren't even valid enough to acknowledge. But as much as I didn't want to admit it, it hurt when things didn't go the way I wanted. It hurt because it mattered, even if I didn't want it to or wished it hadn't. Yet, by telling myself to let go, or rewriting the experience in favor of how I thought I should have felt or reacted, I was invalidating my feelings and, by extension, myself.

Can't Let You Go

The Shit that happened to me was the highlight reel of how I was not *good enough*. But in telling myself to let it go, rather than recognizing that I was hurt and dealing with it, I hurt myself far more. I wasn't seeing all that I could create because I was too busy trying not to create the Shit again. And in focusing on what I didn't want, I denied myself the chance to experience what I did.

By assuring myself that letting go was the answer to my problems, I moved away from, not closer to, the relationship I'd always wanted—the one with myself. But that is what letting go tells us to do—to forget who we are, to scrub all the parts of our history that we'd prefer never happened, and most of all, to erase the fact that we made the wrong choice in the first place.

Moreover, in expecting that as my external situation changed, my internal one would follow suit, I made every interaction a matter of life and death whilst simultaneously trying to ensure my survival. I may have told myself that I'd be rewarded with the perfect relationship to mirror my perfect healing practice, but what I was actually expecting (and experiencing) was more heartbreak because it was all that I'd known.

Even if I'd used my past as a testament to how far I'd come, it would have continued to define me because I would have measured myself against everything I'd overcome. I would have looked for the silver lining whilst pretending that my pain was for the best—further cementing the misguided belief that the only way I could experience joy was if pain preceded it. But brushing my Shit off with excuses that it was for the best or that it was necessary for my growth and evolution wouldn't make it go anywhere. Instead, I split myself into parts: the person who could be satisfied with so little whilst also wanting more; the person who kept dating whilst hiding who she was; and the person who promised herself that one more disappointment would mean the end but kept expecting disappointment, so that's all she ever experienced.

That's the thing about expectations. They hurt us just as much as our Shitty stories. When we approach situations from expectations, we create situations and scenarios to fulfill them, even if they're just in our heads. I'd been coming at everything from my mind rather than my heart—meeting someone whilst bracing myself for a fall, opening up whilst on red alert for heartbreak, and feeling like someone was important to me whilst freaking out because I didn't trust what that meant.

We spend so much of our lives responding and reacting to our Shit that we make it the only reality we know. Of course, it's far easier to ignore our pain by telling ourselves that we can just let it go, blaming someone else (and their problems) for our misfortune, cursing the gods, and burying our heads in the sand. But it's not some god, or even another person, who's the reason why we don't feel *good enough*. It's us. And the longer we disbelieve and avoid facing that truth, the more we actualize the ultimate self-fulfilling prophecy.

In putting pressure on my relationships to be different from the previous ones, I ensured they would be the same. All it took was a longer reply to a text, an offhand comment, or a slight look to take me back to where I started, expecting history to repeat itself whilst trying to mitigate it. So with no other explanation, I concluded that my heart didn't know best after all and that I couldn't expect anything other than disappointment—not because I didn't have any feelings but because I didn't want them to let me down again. So when it inevitably happened, without any other obvious reason, I could only blame myself. It hadn't worked out because I was unlovable.

Although I kept telling myself that I wasn't *good enough*, the opposite had always been the truth. Sure, things may not have turned out the way I thought they would, but until I could see the end of the story, judging myself in the middle was never going to work out in my favor. But, in denying the parts of me that made me who I am, I distorted that truth until I couldn't recognize myself. I hadn't been the problem, but in believing that I was, I turned myself into one, to the point that I disliked what I saw in the mirror—thus ensuring that everything I saw was tainted by my karma rather than the belief that my life could be more.

Letting go wasn't the answer. It was the problem. By dismissing my experiences and the feelings that resulted, I was also dismissing the beliefs that underpinned them. I wasn't just rejecting the experiences that hurt, I was rejecting my ability to do anything about it. And whilst I may not have been able to change the outcome, in letting go entirely of my situation and all the feelings that went with it, I ensured nothing would change because I had nothing left to build from.

I may have been excited to let go of the shame that I was unlovable, but I was also letting go of the faith that told me I could be more than my karmic story. I may have been grateful to let go of the humiliation of my disappointments, but I was also letting go of the trust that I could always share my love and be loved by someone else in return. I may have been relieved to let go of the pain, but I was also letting go of the knowing that it didn't have to be that way. In my need to forget all the things that had hurt, I was also trying to forget all the things that made me unique. And I was letting go of something that mattered… me.

By distancing myself from who I was, I diminished my power. I destroyed the connection within until I forgot who I was. That's why, when I changed my approach, I also changed everything. In finding the courage to follow my heart and allowing my mind to see it working out, I rebuilt the connection within myself. Because every time I chose myself over my fears, I was also choosing to believe that I was *good enough* to make that choice. Instead of repeating the same patterns, I did what I hadn't been able to do since I was a child, which was to be myself regardless of the perceived consequences. I was also picking up a piece of myself that I'd left behind.

When we tell ourselves we're not *good enough*, or that we can only be *good enough* when someone else says so, it hurts. And when we tell ourselves that we can never be *good enough*, it hurts even more. So, if I wanted to stop hurting, I had to stop hurting myself. The only thing that had ever been holding me back was my belief that I wasn't *good enough* to make my own choices or exercise what I believed was best for me. But when I said yes (and meant it), I was healing all the times when I didn't have the courage to permit myself to do so. When I allowed the possibilities of that yes to unfold, I was healing the belief that I couldn't choose for my highest good.

All the things that made me different were my strengths and all the aspects of myself that I had denied were actually the ones that were helping me create the life that I desired. Seeing it in action allowed me to heal the belief that it wasn't possible for me because I could finally recognize that I was the only one who could facilitate it. And when I was able to look back and see what I had created as a result of all my choices, I saw that my fear of being unlovable was actually the one thing holding me back, especially when I understood that the key to everything that I had ever wanted was Love.

Love was the key to mastering my Shit, and listening to my heart facilitated it. When I permitted myself to follow my heart, I was actually reverting to my natural state. I was choosing to hope, have faith in myself, trust that I could always create the life I desired, and know that it was possible. That meant every choice I made was in Love and that the results of that choice would always mirror that Love.

Love had always been the key, but I lived in its absence rather than its presence. And the one thing that differentiated love from Love was whether I was making a choice between fear and the commitment to myself that I would never again betray who I was for another. In choosing myself, I chose Love and everything that Love could do for me. In living by my own rules, I realized the life I actually wanted.

Diamond Girl
Liz

For some, there is a reason for *everything*. Either signs are everywhere, and if we pay attention, then we will find the answers to our burning questions, or we can ascribe significance to everything in our lives from the superficial things like manifesting a parking space (see, I was meant to show up here, otherwise I wouldn't have found parking), to more loaded experiences such as someone breaking our hearts or the pain caused by a neglectful parent (that was all meant to teach me how to love myself).

Others believe that life comprises a series of random events to explain away the seemingly needless suffering that comes with being in body on this Earth plane. This allows us to explain away how out of control we feel in our lives, which relinquishes us of responsibility.

Much like the glass-half-empty or glass-half-full perspective doesn't signify a better or worse way to look at life, nor does the random chaos theory matter any more than the signs and their importance. Rather, it's all of the above.

It can all be rather pointless really, unless we recognize it for what it is: our human selves trying to find and assign meaning to our lives through the narrow filters of our minds and experiences. Even the proponents of random chaos are still trying to explain and discover meaning. The end result just matters less to them than those who care about signs. Ultimately, that's what connects us all, our attempt to define and understand what it means to be us, to be human, and to be alive.

And no, it's not love. Not really.

It's been taught that the meaning of life is love. Many of us have spent much of our lives pursuing it, so it must be the case, right? We're so preoccupied with relationships and sex, various forms of connections, and our interdependence as a species, so it has to be the case, right? And if it wasn't for love, we'd be bereft of our sense of selves, of something greater than us, and we'd end up in isolation and self-loathing, right?

No. No. And No.

We're led to believe that love is everything because it's the way to find meaning in a world of polarity and Separation. It's the antidote to the pain and suffering that it brings. If we're being torn apart within or without, then love is the glue that keeps us together. Except it isn't. Rather, it's the meaning and significance we give love that keeps us together, that binds us to the world of Separation and drives us to keep pulling on that rope in the game of tug of war.

Where polarity pulls us in one direction, our focus on love being the end-all of the game pushes us the other way. And it works for as long as it can. Love as a concept, as a force powerful enough to prevent us from imploding from all the grief and misery in our lives, becomes so significant that we think it impossible to live without it. But in needing it the same way we need air, it becomes distorted by our view of it, to the point that it's lost its meaning.

When we say "I love you" to our spouse or lover, what are we really saying? Usually, it's, "I need you," "I want you," or "I cannot live without you." For many, it's the latter. We literally cannot live without the idea that we are being sourced by someone else. Many of us have spent a good deal of our time and energy seeking the One, the person who can help us define our worth by loving us in return. We've turned love into our purpose, distorting the experience even more.

Love, in its most elevated form, is a wondrous thing. It's what enables Oneness consciousness. While it's not everything, it's so powerful that it can certainly seem like it. However, it's the very preponderance of love, our very worship of it in our limited human understanding, that has steered us into this hopeless abyss that many of us feel—so much so that the more conscious we become, and the more awake we are to our karmic themes and stories, the more love seems insufficient.

Love, or rather the meaning attributed to it, is only half the story. What happens after we get to love is really the point, but we miss that because that's what gets left out of the fairy tales and love stories. When looking at the glass half full, what about the half-empty bit? The part ready to be filled? That's been our purpose all along. We just couldn't see it because we were too busy looking for signs or surrendering to the apparent meaninglessness of life. And thanks to our karmic stories, sometimes we're buried too far under the weight of our Shit to see that there's more to life than all of this.

But nothing is real unless we believe it is, and nothing is random. Ultimately, it's up to us and the perspective we choose that dictates how we experience our lives. What matters is that we define that meaning in our lives. Every one of us is here to recognize our purpose and drive that purpose. That's what it means to be powerful. Only when we do this can we understand our collective purpose.

Bring Me To Life

Purpose in its truest form cannot be understood in the 3D framework of Separation because part of what underpins Separation is hierarchy. Purpose has become linked to our survival or reason for living, which it never was. Therefore, purpose cannot be seen as holistic or whole, as it was merely defined as the roles we played in humanity's game to further its growth and evolution.

We've destroyed the concept of purpose by believing that it's quantifiable. We've limited the idea of it by believing that it relates to money, success, or another person. We've damaged our purpose by assuming it relates to a job, career, or relationship. We've allowed it to be defined by other people, either by emulating their success or assuming that we don't have as many choices available to us. So, it's easy to couch our purpose in something more ephemeral, a designation for this lifetime only, and equate it to the work we take on in order to earn an income. But now, as the notion of work is being unthreaded, as people realize that they are more than their flesh and the effort to sustain their mere survival on Earth, we see what our purpose really is.

Purpose is not our reason for living. The reason for living is quite simply to come into our divinity. Divinity in this case means being the most transcendent version or experience that we can attain through full-bodied consciousness; or, more simply put, to realize our unlimited God-selves by traversing the entire spectrum of existence possible; or even more simply put, to experience life to the fullest; or even more simply put beyond that, to live fearlessly in our most creative and powerful form.

Purpose underpins that reason. Since our reason for living is to come into our divinity, purpose is how we choose to express and experience that divinity (we've kept this broad here since it is always up to us to decide how we express our divinity because we are that divine). Where the former is to understand that we are capable of doing anything, the latter is realizing it. But the exact nature of our purpose is not as important as the steps we undergo to prepare for our purpose and to connect to it. There are two reasons why the process matters more than our actual purpose:

1. To develop the courage to remain in our purpose, even when it becomes difficult.

2. To come into a profound sense of personal joy we cannot necessarily develop through relationships with others. That joy breeds an unconditional beingness within ourselves, that is, we cannot manipulate, change, or control who we are when we are living our purpose.

While in Separation, purpose is a role people perform. In Oneness consciousness, purpose is the unique contribution one offers to the collective. In other words, our purpose is to serve. The more Oneness enables us to connect more fully to one another, the more impact these contributions have on the whole of humanity.

The very idea of service may not appeal to most. For some, serving can be regarded as noble, and for others, it can seem like slavery. In a world that has existed within a hierarchical framework, the notion of service presumes that there is a person or group to serve and that they are somehow better than us in status, class, income, or education. This then reinforces the idea that we are, in one way or another, not *good enough.*

Purpose is facilitated by how we process the world around us and the natural gifts we have. How we experience our divinity is unique to us, so how we express that divinity through our purpose is just as unique. Even if we don't believe that there is anything unique about us, often a strong desire or unbending sense of commitment we bring to a personal passion or idea is the arrow pointing us towards fulfillment. Conversely, the more frustrated and angrier we are around our work or in our lives, the more it shows how disconnected we've become from our purpose.

We can better understand how we express our purpose by breaking this down into four categories:

1. Emotional
2. Physical
3. Mental
4. Spiritual

1. Emotional

Emotional purpose signifies that whatever we carry with us into this human life and how we choose to experience this world will be felt at the deepest possible level. Those with an emotional purpose can be empaths, the ones who help humanity divest itself of its fears by bearing the emotional weight of the world (we can have an emotional purpose without being an empath, but it's rare).

They are the friends, caregivers, healers, and helpers who want to wipe our tears and hug us. They are also our teachers and counselors who, with great courage and honesty, share their own emotional experiences with others to open the door for the rest of us to face our own, which is something that many of us are uncomfortable doing. They have the skills to take us step by step through the process of grief, sadness, denial, joy, and even more grief to guide us on our path of self-discovery.

2. Physical

What would our outside world look like if it weren't for those who could realize what others can only dream? Physical purpose manifests our internal worlds. Those with a physical purpose are the people who create our physical reality. They may be architects, builders, engineers, programmers, or artists who project their imaginations and make their inner worlds real. They are the ones who give shape and form to thoughts and ideas. Without them, our world wouldn't contain the mark of divinity that we hold inside ourselves, which is the fullest expression of our souls and thus gives life to all that we create.

3. Mental

The mind isn't all about logic or reason. The mind, utilized to its fullest, is like music. As someone with mental purpose, Rhea explains it as being able to see many moving parts and how those parts slot into place in a way that is reminiscent of a beautiful piece of music with dancing notes. It's math, poetry, creation, and intuition wrapped into one. Those whose purpose is mental grasp the larger picture around their interests and subjects and easily dissect the layers of understanding around them.

They are the ones who connect the dots and simplify complicated concepts.

This isn't exclusive to science or teaching, nor is it only prevalent in politics, government, organizations, NGOs, and public policy. Having a mental purpose allows those to use their analytical minds to develop the deepest possible understanding of any subject, from the arts and sciences to music and technology. The most prominent feature of someone with a mental purpose is their ability to make connections to the multi-faceted nature of our world and disseminate that information to others in a way that everyone can understand.

4. Spiritual

Contrary to popular belief, most with spiritual purpose are not religious, nor do they tend towards any kind of spiritual, religious, or dogmatic belief system. However, they do intuitively understand that our world is an expression of the Divine and all that is within it reflects that. Spiritual purpose transcends our reality, but it always comes back to the source of all life. It is the only one of the four purposes that extends through all four bodies (mental, emotional, physical, and spiritual).

So, while some may relate to one or two of these generalized categories, someone with a true spiritual purpose will cover all four and link them back to the Divine. They need to connect through all four in order to serve humanity because they are meant to reach everyone in the most holistic way possible by speaking to their souls.

It could be that in reading this, some may relate to more than one category. The key is to consider that they explain how we strengthen our connection to our experiences and the world around us. Do we tend to feel our way through something? Would we prefer to jump in and do the job ourselves? Do we crave knowing more about a particular subject? Or are we more inclined to take an entirely different view of life and witness it from every vantage possible?

Becoming a Nun

When we grasp our purpose, the path is much like becoming a nun or joining a monastic order or any other sacred process one undertakes to show devotion to something greater than oneself. It does not mean, however, that we become renunciates by sacrificing the things that bring us joy. On the contrary, it's about displaying devotion to the one thing (not another person, group, or deity) that enables us to serve ourselves as well as the greater good of humanity. In fact, what we do with our purpose is less important than living authentically with that purpose.

While one category may make us adept at a particular job, those who identify with a given category can be a leader, a teacher, a builder, a designer, an entrepreneur, a performer, a healer, a writer, an artist, and so on. It's their unique perspective and passion that they bring which shows their purpose. It helps to have people from all categories in every field because it creates a more holistic experience for the person serving and for those benefiting. It also means that together we can combine our perspectives and experience the most expanded view of our lives and the world.

Purpose is joy, as in, follow the joy and find your purpose. This is particularly important as we make this move from Separation to Oneness because what careers we choose may not be tied entirely to our purpose. It may be that we need a day job to support a hobby or passion project that brings us joy. Perhaps that hobby will grow into something more and direct us towards something beyond anything we could have envisioned. It may be that we have personal issues, fears, phobias, hang-ups, or relationships that we need to heal before discovering what brings us joy and pursuing it with our hearts. And that's what it takes to determine our joy—a connection to our hearts.

Hearts are our joy meters. When we love, cherish, adore, connect, like, or feel anything on that spectrum, we come closer to pinpointing that which brings us joy. The more we operate from our hearts, the greater our capacity to feel our way through life, which opens our hearts wider. And the more open they are, the closer we come to our purpose. This takes confronting all those issues and karma that keep us in Separation.

It also demands that we divest ourselves of all the fears that trap us within the perceived limitations of our human existence. Fear is the biggest block to our truth (which is that we are the Divine), and without truth, we cannot see our purpose for what it is. That means we must take responsibility for who we are, our choices, and especially our fate. It's not a simple task to readily accept our purpose, to see ourselves in our most God-like manner, or to recognize our divinity and ability to serve ourselves and others—nor is it easy to look in the mirror and see that we are far more than we perceive ourselves to be.

Becoming our fullest and most divine selves is a step-by-step process. First, it requires us to want something greater for ourselves than the things we've been conditioned to accept as enough. Second, we must recognize that only we can provide it for ourselves. And third, we have to believe we can realize it in this lifetime.

When We Were Young
Liz

No one likes to suffer. No one enjoys pain. But most of all, no one likes to suffer at the hands of their own choices.

In the last twenty years, I developed an autoimmune disorder, had postpartum depression, experienced tremendous bouts of stress moving countries, felt like a single mother for most of my children's early years, and never really put my degrees or education to any kind of practical use. To believe that I caused my own suffering was, at times, too much to bear. But every time I wanted to blame someone else for my own hurt, I heard my mentor's words when I was eighteen, lost, and angry: "Remember, you chose this life, and *everything* that goes with it." While deep down, I knew this was true, I couldn't fully comprehend *why*. If I chose *all* of the Shit, *why* didn't I make smarter choices?

The problem is that when we only have ourselves to blame, we only have ourselves to punish. What my mentor couldn't teach me, and what no one can ever really teach, is how to avoid the mines, since life in our karma is one big minefield. No one can mentor us through self-effacing, self-destructive behaviors. Learning how to navigate comes with experience and a series of trial and error because our karma sets different traps.

The only takeaway advice I received later was to "Elevate every experience as a lesson, not only because you chose it but because it's meant to teach you something about the Divine." In other words, keep your eyes, ears, mind, and heart open. Always the attentive student, I applied what he taught to the best of my ability, but it wasn't easy.

In the end, whatever I went through, the burden of responsibility was always on me. No matter what unfolded in my life, I was always the author of it. No matter what happened, I was ultimately the protagonist of my story. The moral of the entire story, both written and unfinished, is that since I was the only one who chose my story, I was the only one who could choose how it played out.

That meant that I had to pay attention to each and every one of my choices and process and learn from the lessons. This didn't involve breaking down and analyzing everything or making lists to manifest or improve anything to attain some outward goal or wish. All it required was that I become more conscious of myself.

There were two things that I understood intuitively since being a young girl. The first was that I had the answers to my questions, so no one could teach me anything I didn't already know. The second was that not only was I here for a reason, but I was also here for a *reason*. My mentor helped me discover the connection from my intuition to the pain of my lessons, and how they not only brought me back to a deeper understanding of myself but how that understanding would lead me to my purpose. The more aware of myself I became, the clearer my motivations, purpose, and life path would become— the sum of which made up my fate.

But it wasn't that simple. I had karma too. So, while I was moving towards what I thought was my fate (maybe pursue a Ph.D. and teach, or maybe try my hand at magazine publishing), I was ignoring what my frustrated attempts were telling me. I became so locked in the notion that I needed to prove my worth and earn my living that I neglected to see that I was actually living a life that suited me.

I was allowed the time and space to connect to my dormant spiritual skills, all the while experiencing different cultures and learning about love and commitment with my partner. But the fact that it didn't match up to the image in my mind created such a dissonance that I struggled to make peace with it for a long time.

The irony is that, since the age of nineteen, I knew what I was going to do with my life, which is what I'm doing today. It became crystal clear the moment I sat across from a spiritual advisor (Ellen Kaufman Dosick, for anyone who listens to the podcast) and asked what I should be concentrating on in college. In asking, "What am I going to do with the rest of my life?" I was actually asking the bigger question: "What am I here to do?"

Before Ellen uttered a word, my immediate thought was, "I'm going to do what you do one day." But my limited mind said it would be later after I've had a real job (the hubris and wisdom of youth summed up in a single sentence). Except when the real job never materialized, and I wound up taking what felt like a massive detour over continents, a part of me wondered when my purpose would begin.

Out Of Time

While many struggle to grasp the answer to *what*, *how*, or *why*, it's the *when* that confounds most. Time is truly the mother of all struggles. Our relationship with Time fucks us up in the worst ways. To operate and survive within the framework of Separation, we need guidelines and structure. This order helps us make sense of our lives, co-exist with others, anticipate outcomes, and strive for easy goals. The problem is that it gives us a warped sense of time, where everything has to be done within a particular timeframe or it won't happen at all. And if it doesn't happen, or if it does, but not in the way it was supposed to, then it implies that we're failing in some way, reinforcing once again that we're not *good enough*.

Turning eighteen means we become adults and are expected to make our way out into the world. Maybe we should go to university or find a vocation. By 30, many are married and have children. By 50 or 60, our productive years are generally finished. Even though we've seen these ideas shift tremendously over the past two decades, we're still dealing with the echoes of our damaged relationship with Time.

Time doesn't rule us, nor are we in control of it. Rather, we are the agents of Time, which means we work with its benevolent energy, which was always intended to keep our growth and evolution on a forward trajectory, avoiding regression or devolution. (This book doesn't address the space-time continuum or multi-dimensional existence because it isn't necessary for this karmic discussion.)

The greater our relationship with Time, the less we are ruled by it. The more we evolve and the closer to our purpose we get, the less significant Time becomes. Because Time isn't about schedules or agendas or outward goals of achievement. Instead, its function is to connect the moments of learning that prepare us for realizing our larger fate.

Time, in this case, is a growth opportunity. This is why many of us have a love-hate (but mostly hate) relationship with Time. We're almost always feeling too late, far behind, or out of time altogether, and it makes us resent it. But our being late or not showing up has nothing to do with Time. It has everything to do with whether or not we're taking the opportunities our karmic issues present to us for growth (which is why many of us struggle with those outward expectations of milestones marked by years and age).

When we put off these moments of learning, we feel punished by Time because the other things failed to show (those being the more fun and exciting events we anticipate because we all sense we're here for a reason). And the more punished and resentful we feel, the less motivated we are to do anything about it because we feel too powerless to change anything, especially our fate. But when this happens, the karmic issue takes over and piles on the Shit—not to put us at a greater disadvantage but to wake us up.

As a result, we often wind up conflating our fate with our karma. We might convince ourselves that we drew the short straw in life or tell ourselves that it wasn't in the cards. Unfortunately, in denying our sense of being and our belonging here for a reason, we push ourselves further away from our purpose and, as a result, ourselves. But the further away from ourselves we veer, the further from our hearts we get and we become disassociated with Time until it ceases to be on our side and becomes our enemy.

In which case, Time stretches interminably before us, mirroring that vast emptiness we created inside by existing outside of ourselves. So, when our karma finally awakens us, we are suddenly aware of this space that we need to traverse to get back to ourselves, and it can be intimidating. It may appear that it would take us forever to get to our desired destination, and it may not seem possible. That's when we are most inclined to give up and assure ourselves with sentiments like "maybe in the next life" or "it wasn't meant to be."

But we *are* meant to be. Our desires, our passions, and our joys are meant to exist. They are meant to take up residence in our physical world and nurture us as we embrace our purpose. We just need to recognize that while karma aids us by directing us to our purpose, which serves our fate, fate itself supersedes our karma. So, whatever our karmic themes and lessons are, we are not meant to be kept from our fate any longer than is necessary to resolve and heal our issues.

The problem is that most of us have allowed our issues to persist beyond their expiration date. The reason for this is two-fold. First, there isn't enough emotional support to manage the healing process. Second, the discomfort of the karmic issue makes us push it off to the point where we deny that our karma exists at all. But if we can hold enough Oneness consciousness, even if we're still burning through our karma, we can imagine or even fathom that we are, in one form or another, connected to something larger. And being a part of this larger framework means we function within this universe where all living beings are connected by life force.

The greater our connection to this universe, the clearer we are about our fate. This is because fate isn't just about our personal stories or our purpose, it's also about the greater context in which our stories play out—because we do not exist within a vacuum. Our stories impact others and their stories, which are intertwined with ours, across and throughout Time and dimension. They are part and parcel of a large thread of our existence that spans eons of human and soul evolution. Confused yet? That's okay. This is merely a glimpse of a corner of the wider tapestry of our divine existence and how this karmic play we're acting out is such a small bit of something so damn big.

Right on Track

When we realize our connection to the universe, we can be clearer about our fate because that fate extends beyond our limited human selves and connects us to that larger tapestry of existence. And in connecting to our fate, everything and everyone associated with that fate conspires to get us where we need to be. It may not be an active effort on anyone's part. It could be as simple as someone setting an intention or expressing a need for a specific talent that only we can provide as designed by our purpose. It could be the result of a desire, whether ours or someone else's (whose purpose is so entwined with ours), that we are needed in order to help fully realize it. Whatever our fates hold, we must understand they are not ours to maintain or fulfill alone, but they are a huge part of enabling the leap of our human consciousness into divine knowing.

The challenge is that the longer we are in service to our karma, and the more we allow it to rule our lives and perspectives, the longer we remain from actualizing our fate to its fullest potential. And the longer we remain stuck, the more fucked we are when it comes to Time because it literally and figuratively gets away from us, until we feel so far away from where we started, and so removed from ourselves, that many of us just want to give up entirely and say, "fuck it."

But we're not here for a "fuck it" moment, we're here to say, "Fuck This." Fuck the old, decrepit systems and relationship paradigms that don't serve us. Fuck the self-serving bureaucracies and governments. Fuck the bullshit philosophies that tell me I have to pay my dues. Fuck anything or anyone who told others they weren't worthy. Fuck all of this and the rest. Fuck karma. While we've needed it, we don't need life to hurt anymore.

The only way to do this is to look ourselves in the mirror and ask, "Who the fuck am I?"

While it's true that we are more complex than we give ourselves credit for, the last thing we need to be doing is denying who we are; from the flesh that envelopes us to the blood running through our veins; or the sex that compels us to connect and enjoy the life force that results; to the annoying monkey on our backs that constantly reminds us of our past heartbreaks, disappointments, and rejections.

Everything about us, from what we wear on the surface to what resides in our hearts, is who we are. And it hurts so much to feel stuck—stuck in an old paradigm where we're wrong, imperfect, and stupid, which has convinced us we're incapable, incompetent, and impotent. The sooner we truly accept that, the sooner we can transcend the bullshit and accept our fate.

At some point, we're meant to transcend our suffering and discomforts, but the only way to do that is to stop resisting or ignoring that they exist. We could never do this by surrendering to them; we must acknowledge that their existence and that the way it was all designed has caused us such pain that we can't live with it any longer. It's not by giving up that we overcome our issues but by embracing them and forgiving ourselves for having chosen them.

For every single one of us, karma is our living hell. What keeps us moving through it is knowing that somehow, at some point, it will get better. While it may sound like human folly to believe something so prosaic, in the end, it's always true. Something will inevitably end our suffering, even if it's death. But this is the lifetime when death and resurrection are certainly possible, just not in the way that people and religions have conceived them.

In our case, we can die several times in a single lifetime and come back with less ego, less pain, and more in touch with our divinity. With every lesson, we can divest ourselves of enough karma that we are truly like new people. And with the courage attained through the very experience of dying and the strength of renewal, we can really say we've been to hell and back and come out the other side.

This is the lifetime to end all suffering—not because karma won't continue to exist but because we're coming to a point in our evolution where ending our suffering won't handicap or paralyze us. We can finally see how it can direct us to our purpose and bring us into the compassion required to realize Oneness consciousness. First, we have to own the fact that we chose our fate and, as a result, all the pains our choices involve. Second, we have to step into our purpose. This can only be enabled when we've resolved enough of our hurts to recognize that beneath everything is a greater potential waiting to be unleashed.

Waiting On the World to Change
Rhea

Ever since I was young, there have been a few things that felt very important to me. First, I was fascinated with relationships, which will be of no surprise to anyone reading this book or anyone who has listened to our podcasts. Whether it was the Disney princesses or simply watching a tender moment between my parents, I knew that our connections with each other are to be treasured, to be enjoyed, and are fucking important.

Second (again, unsurprisingly), I knew things could be done differently from how they had been done before. Whether it was challenging a concept that others took for granted or offering an alternative solution, I realized things didn't have to be how they always were.

Third, I knew that love was going to be the key to my purpose and fate. I never worried about how my life was going to unfold, however, or if it was all going to work out. I just knew, at the very bottom of my heart, that I was going to make a difference in the world.

What I didn't account for was karma. Whilst in my youth, it may have been easy for me to exist in a state where I was enough, but the second I started interacting with others, that shifted. Wherever I turned and whatever

I did, there was always someone telling me that my outlook, my approach, or my knowing was wrong. And the more I saw it, heard it, and experienced it, the more I internalized that judgment—to the point where I thought my life didn't matter at all. It felt like there wasn't anything that needed to change in the world, apart from me. For someone who knew that relationships were the key to joy, I had allowed them to destroy me and sever the most important one I had: the relationship with myself.

The moment we stop seeing ourselves as *good enough* is when life goes sideways. When we can't think for ourselves, listen to ourselves, and ultimately be ourselves, we end up compounding our fears. We create a world full of self-fulfilling prophecies that narrows our possibilities over and over again until it seems as if there is only one path for us to choose. But the longer we believe that we are not *good enough*—which underpins everything we say, think, or do—the more sideways it goes until we are completely upside down.

It can take us a long time to realize we are upside down. In hiding out in a budding embroidery addiction, and living vicariously through other people, I stopped giving my life any purpose. I may have thought I was being patient, or waiting for the good things to come, but I was actually avoiding my fear that I was unlovable. Thing is, my fear couldn't go anywhere if I couldn't face it, which meant that I couldn't get very far. So, in looking for validation from someone else, all I uncovered were increasingly imaginative reflections of the ways in which I had decided I wasn't *good enough*.

I was in a hell of my own making, doomed to experience relationships that were a manifestation of my fears and insecurities. I had also effectively destroyed the things that mattered to me by telling myself that I didn't matter. But in telling myself that I didn't matter, I was negating the very power that came with being me. Turns out that to really know how powerful I was, I had to understand how I made myself powerless.

I had kept myself powerless because I didn't want to take responsibility for my life. Except in refusing to acknowledge how every single one of my choices contributed to my disempowerment, I kept myself waiting—waiting for my life to start, waiting for some expert to save me, waiting for the right crystal to find me, waiting for the universe to forgive me, waiting to meet the perfect partner, and waiting to discover the reason for all my pain. But until I woke the fuck up and said "Fuck This," all my waiting was in vain.

It's My Life

I know what hopelessness feels like. It's rock bottom, there are no more moves left to play, no more chances left to take, and a total engulfment of apathy. It's the "I can't feel anymore…" or "I don't care anymore…" or "I don't want anymore…" because we've been disappointed so many times that we just don't have the energy to believe something different. It's in the acceptance that life just isn't what we believed it could be, and there is nothing we can do about it, no matter what we try. It's deeper than *I Am not Good Enough.* It's the understanding that we have nothing to lose and no more excuses or reasons or barriers telling us not to take a risk. It's two words, and those words are simple.

"Fuck This."

What we don't realize is just how powerful those two words are. We have conditioned ourselves to believe pain is the only life we will know. But in saying "Fuck This," we recognize that we've had enough, even in the smallest of ways. We are done with the hurt, and we are fed up with searching for meaning in our suffering. Thing is, only we can decide when we are ready to own our lives.

When I finally had enough of my pain, I made that choice—and not because I couldn't stand it anymore or because some well-meaning friend who wanted to see me "reach my full potential and level up my worth" gave me a tough-love speech. It was because I had finally accepted that living like everyone else wasn't going to work for me.

But even though saying "Fuck This" may have been the bravest choice I'd made thus far, what I was effectively doing was course-correcting. Just as the choice to believe everyone else's hype had led to a whole host of other choices that caused me to lose myself, the opposite choice required the same process to bring me back to myself.

That meant that every subsequent choice had to come from me when I was ready. No amount of external or internal force could have pushed me to make them sooner, and I could never take a shortcut, otherwise, I would find myself going back. I wasn't just learning what my Shit was showing me (to own my power, or as Liz says, my divinity), but I was also developing the one thing that was going to carry me along my path: trust. I was remembering to trust that I was capable of living my life for me, as me.

Experiencing how powerful we really are takes listening to all our secret thoughts, feelings, wisdom, and passion. It takes following our intuition, no matter the potential consequences or how crazy it seems. Now, I can't lie; it requires some practice because we don't know how to do this automatically, and everything in our society has taught us to do the opposite. More often than not, in the beginning, we learn all the ways in which we've given up our power. But the more we give room for our power to grow and intensify, the more everything that we do, say, and believe becomes an extension of that power—bringing us closer to realizing our greater goal, which is to be happy.

Yet, happiness isn't possible if we skirt around our power by pretending, lying, and morphing our lives to simulate some external idea of what it should be. Happiness depends upon remembering who we are, connecting to what brings us joy, and expressing it all to our fullest potential—because no one else can define who we are, so they cannot define our happiness either. That's why the more we exercise Love and pursue what we actually want, rather than settle for the socially constructed bullshit we think we deserve, the more we allow that joy to unfold. And when we follow that joy, wherever it leads, nothing and no one can stop us from living our greatest happiness.

Into the Unknown
Liz

We are in a time when we have nothing else to push against except ourselves. We've finally been gifted the opportunity to face ourselves and recognize that throughout history, the only enemy we were really fighting was us. But it isn't easy to lay down our arms and embrace ourselves, not when we've been in Separation for so long.

Healing ourselves requires a series of manageable steps. We don't just wake up to our karma and will ourselves into Oneness. If that were the case, the world would appear a lot different. Instead, to bridge the gap between Separation and Oneness, we must come into Oneness within ourselves.

That's truly the most challenging process of all because the moment we decide to improve our lives and change what isn't working is when the real work actually begins. Because everything up until that very second was our karma pushing, poking, and prodding us to wake up. All the discontentment, aches, pains, discomfort, and joylessness we were experiencing were mere preludes to coming into our purpose, which is only part of the picture.

To survive Separation, we need to remain smaller versions of ourselves. Fear drives us to hide, seek shelter under someone else's umbrella, and wait out the storm. Except the storm never passes, and we wind up waiting for so long that we watch as others pass us, fearlessly weathering what comes their way, until one day we wake up and ask ourselves, "What have I done with my life?"

Choosing ourselves, and the opportunities that rest outside of what our limited minds can conceive, requires a level of faith that absolutely ANYTHING can happen. The idea that ANYTHING can happen strikes terror in most because we fear the fallout. But if we look back into the past, up until now, despite all the destruction, wars, famines, and bullshit, we are here. We are living, breathing humans who have survived and endured a great deal. And we are still standing. Yet we continue to doubt. We continue to fear. We are gifted when it comes to second-guessing. We are geniuses when assigning blame. We continue to question and double back on decisions "just in case." We are incredibly talented when it comes to hedging, even on bets where we have no skin in the game. Most of all, we are truly masters of the art of punishment.

The first step to our healing is to grasp what our karmic theme is. It's the story that feeds our Separation, that keeps us feeling small, and whispers in our ear at the most inopportune time that we are not *good enough*. It reveals itself through our relationships, not just our families or lovers, but coworkers, teachers, friends, and even our relationships with entities such as our employers, schools, or organizations. So when we find ourselves triggered, stressed, worried, overwhelmed, anxious, or miserable, we're being shown where our karmic issues lie.

This brings us to the second step, and probably one of the most challenging. We need to bear witness to how we've destroyed ourselves, which is essentially walking into our own version of hell. And yet, it's the only way. Mindfulness, gratitude, manifestation, self-help gurus, spiritual influencers, diets, and workouts will not help us pass through the door. Some won't even show us the actual door and instead will present us with an imitation, making us believe that we are doing just enough to get by.

We only know we're tackling our karmic themes when we hit bottom, Go Dark, and are forced to be honest about how our choices are literally and figuratively killing us, hurting our hearts, damaging our self-esteem, and ruining our bodies. Bearing witness demands that we humbly accept that we alone are responsible for all of our choices and that we admit we didn't know any better— not because we're not in control of our fate, or that we're just plain thick, but because to really learn something, we need to answer the question, "Is this all there is?"

If we don't get it on the first or second try, it doesn't mean we've failed. We don't fail. Ever. We all require a series of opportunities to help us reach the multitudinous levels of our divine wisdom. And that takes Time. So, to bear witness does not mean to watch with detachment. Rather, it means allowing ourselves to experience and feel what we are going through to the best of our ability, all the while being completely and utterly self-aware. If we try to disassociate ourselves from the theme, the karmic issue doesn't heal entirely.

We treat karma like a game of life or death because it is. While it's natural for our karma to compel us to act self-destructively, the gift of that self-destruction is the third step, the death of all we've ever known. In holding onto our fear of death, we keep ourselves from actually experiencing life. We cause our own paralysis and we create our own purgatory, neither living in joy nor seeing that hell is merely our fears manifested.

If we embrace our death with compassion, we can accept that our carefully constructed and curated world was our ego's attempt to help us survive and keep us safe in Separation. This is the most fundamental step in coming into ourselves and sometimes the scariest one because all that's left to ask ourselves is, "What's next?"

Burning our bridges to our past misery, shame, and fear drives us towards the next step, which few have actually been able to do. Most of us spend a great deal of our lives in our karmic loops. But once we've come through our personal hell, the fourth step is to enter the Void. The Void is the space of pure potential. The key to experiencing the Void is understanding that everything is possible when we are in it because the Void contains all the building blocks of information necessary for us to live out our fate. And because it is unique to us, each of these building blocks carries a mark that matches our specific vibration or energy, meaning only we can access this information for ourselves.

While this may seem rather esoteric, unachievable, or just plain weird, there's another way to look at it. From the moment we've healed our karmic theme and glimpsed our purpose (discovering that which brings us immense joy), we realize there are a host of things outside of our imaginations that we have yet to understand. Driven by desire, curiosity, or the intention to find meaning or make sense of something we feel passionate about, we may deep dive into a particular practice, learning, or understanding. Or we may seek to develop skills that we previously convinced ourselves were unattainable in this lifetime.

It could be something as simple as playing an instrument or taking up an art, or perhaps something more labor intensive, such as writing a book or traveling abroad and learning a language. It could also mean going back to school to get a degree or changing career paths. The list of possibilities goes on and on because we are truly capable of anything.

What's important to understand about this step is that, given our limited human perceptions and experience, so much potential can be intimidating. We tend to apply concepts from Separation and create expectations around our purpose, such as deriving an income from it or assuming that it will be the only thing we do with our lives until we die. But the thing about purpose, and the potential that enables it, is that it is limitless. And because the Void is infinite space, all knowledge that we can access becomes infinite as well.

So, our experiences know no bounds, meaning we can keep creating and doing, creating some more and learning more and expanding, and so on without end. We no longer have to delineate our lives according to phases of artificial time constructs. We can just exist within the larger framework of potential and purpose and living and breathing and existing all within the vast universe in which we reside. All we have to do is release ourselves from expectations so that we can remain open to the potential within the Void.

This doesn't mean seeking the next thing every time we finish a passion project, nor are we supposed to occupy our energies by constantly accessing information. We are not here to sit on mountaintops and contemplate our existence. We are here to create that existence, to give it our energy, and to create a momentum that furthers our consciousness. That is how we evolve, and that is how we change the world.

The only way to do this is with integrity. To live with integrity is to live according to the tenets of our purpose. In other words, to be our fullest, most divine selves so that no matter what happens, we will never deviate from that purpose. And it's with integrity that we can enter the Heart of God. When we've enabled full integrity, we've reached the fifth step, which is to walk the Way of the Master. Don't worry; not all get there in this lifetime.

Fully mastering anything requires a ton of energy, focus, and Time, and we have enough on our plates. However, it is essential to understand that there is no true end to our evolution—that every step we make towards healing our Shit, and every step after as we uncover our purpose, is a step towards mastery. So, just as much as we are learning about who we are at our core, and just as much as we are grasping how connected we are at that very core, we are also coming into mastery over that knowledge. And because we are here to grow and evolve, once we have mastered that knowledge, we will encounter other opportunities for learning and thus mastering something new.

To master our learning demands that the healing and understanding we've developed in this lifetime penetrates all of our bodies (physical, mental, emotional, and spiritual). This is why it can take years. And it may be that while some are mastering esoteric or spiritual ideas associated with the Divine, others may be mastering the art of navigating the world of material concepts. There are multiple facets of being and existing in this world, which means there are a multitude of unique ways in which we can apply our talents and skills.

It can feel like the most impossible, unbridgeable task to heal ourselves and come out feeling whole, without our bullshit and stories chipping away at us. Yet, as much as it's human nature to plateau and resist change, it's also in our nature to want more and to evolve. That's what the whole karmic game was designed to teach us all along— that beyond all the stories we've invented to underscore our Separation, there was a larger intention at play—to come into our divinity.

Once we understand this at our very core, we won't need karma to teach us about ourselves or direct us to our purpose. Instead, we can simply access the power that being in divine space enables and create a new life for ourselves; one that is free of misery, pain, heartache, and dis-ease, all of which can only be realized by us and no one else. How fucking amazing is that?

About KMB

Rhea always had a strong desire to seek justice. Whether it was through learning about law, or working on the team that criminalized coercive control, she never stopped trying to help others. It wasn't until after a few life hiccups that she understood the most effective way to help others was to transform her life first. A podcast and several books about karma, magic and following your heart later, she figured out how to create her own happiness and how to teach others to do the same.

With nearly twenty years' experience as a spiritual advisor to clients around the world, Liz is a medium and Soul Memory Discovery facilitator, who also writes steamy novels under the pen name Vivian Winslow. Her work taught her that despite our surface differences, people are driven by two essential things: a need for love and a desire to find meaning.

Together they created Karma Magic Bliss (or KMB for short) to offer all the tools and information to allow people to realize the lives they desire. This includes free resources (the podcast Karma's My Bitch) as well as in-depth explanations (the books) and practical learning material. To find out more about KMB and what's to come, you can visit www.wearekmb.com or just drop a line through @karmamagicbliss on all social platforms.

Acknowledgments

Writing these acknowledgments has been a long time coming. We started this book in 2019, and the world looked a lot different back then. At the time, we had no idea what this book would say, how many would be in the series, and where we would end up. Four years later, we have finally arrived, and we can't wait to keep going.

Working on this, and with each other, has been a gift. Together, we haven't just created something that we are so fundamentally proud of, but we also learned what it means to work and grow with each other. Despite the numerous eye-rolls from Liz and groans from Rhea when we realized we needed to redraft the same chapter for the eighth time (Chapter Fourteen, in case you were wondering), these books, and the Guidance within them, have changed our lives in indescribable ways.

We want to thank everyone who helped us get here; from Ricardo and Iva, who read the first drafts of the first chapters, to the rest of our family and friends who supported us when we needed perspective or just a little laugh to keep going. Michael and Gabriela, thank you for giving us the space to figure out what we were doing and providing great insight. Thank you to our parents and siblings, who may not have always understood what we were doing but supported us anyway. This wouldn't have been possible without you.

To Tommy, our editor, who didn't just edit the work but pushed us to clarify and explain when we didn't, thank you. You were the first person who read the book in its entirety, and your feedback has elevated this book in so many ways. Kam, our amazing book cover designer, the gradient you created for us wasn't just beautiful, it was exactly what we needed. Thank you for bringing our book to life in a way that only you could. Thank you to those who helped us get off the ground, such as Lara H. who showed Rhea the door into the dance class where she met Liz; Amelia, who lent us our first microphone and suggested Liz's laundry room as our recording studio (thank goodness we've evolved since then); and thank you, Chiara, who became more than a Pilates teacher— we are so happy to count you as a friend like you count our hundreds.

Finally, we want to thank the dating apps that used to live on Rhea's phone. If it wasn't for you, she wouldn't have met the perfect people at the perfect times with the perfect skills. The first chapters would have also been a lot less interesting.

There are more anecdotes and teachings to come: A Karmic Affair (how karma can transform your relationships) and A Karmic Adventure (how karma can trans-form your world) will be released in 2024. But of course, we don't stop at karma. Stay tuned for Magic and Bliss.